ABOUT THE *EXPLORE* SERIES

Since 1888, *National Geographic* magazine has provided its readers a wealth of information and helped us understand the world in which we live. Insightful articles, supported by gorgeous photography and impeccable research, bring the mission of the National Geographic Society front and center: to inspire people to care about the planet. The *Explore* series delivers *National Geographic* to you in the same spirit. Each of the books in this series presents the best articles on popular and relevant topics in an accessible format. In addition, each book highlights the work of National Geographic Explorers, photographers, and writers. Explore the world of *National Geographic*. You will be inspired.

ON THE COVER
Pillars of Göbekli Tepe, the world's oldest temple, in Turkey

ARCHAEOLOGY

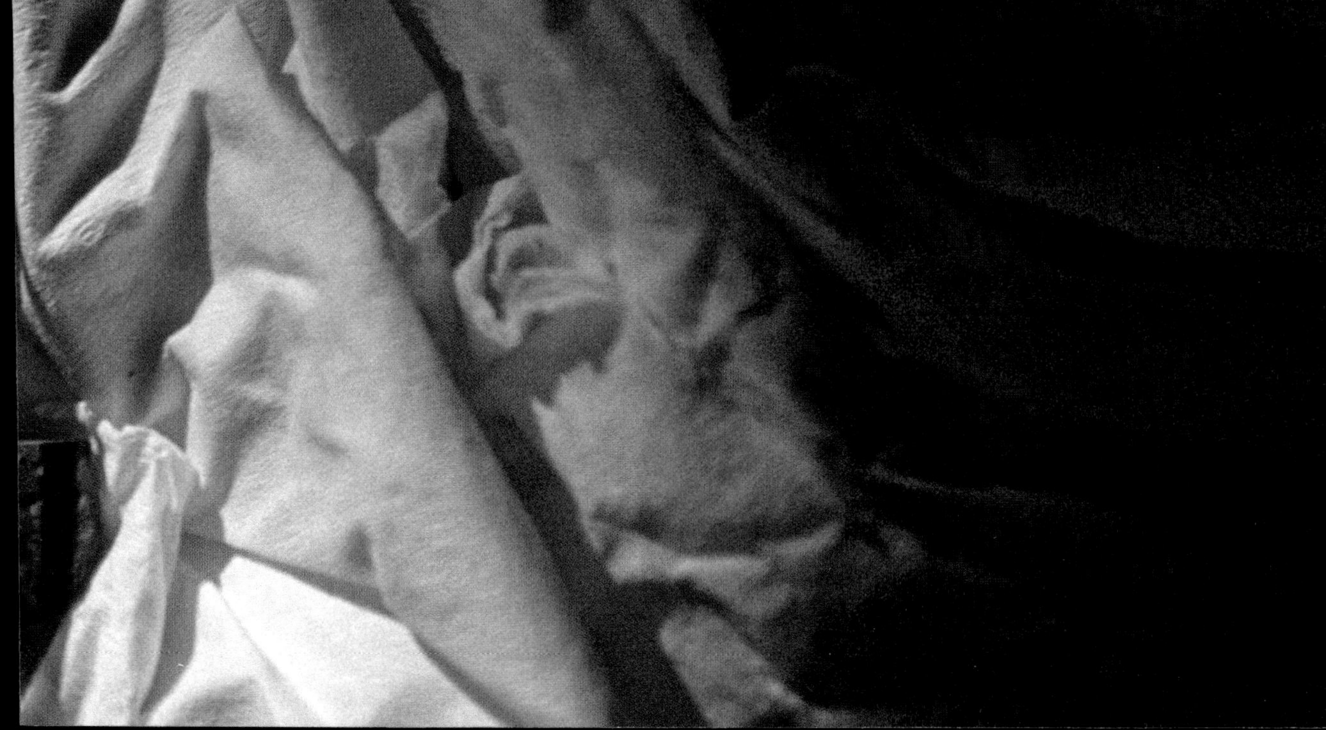

First-century ivory figure discovered in Afghanistan.

In the late 19th century, one man's amateurish act brought about the loss of invaluable artifacts in northwestern Turkey. This tragic loss is still felt by archaeologists today. Heinrich Schliemann was a German businessman with no formal training as an archaeologist. As a hobby, he decided to excavate a site that he believed to be the ancient city of Troy. The city was a central part of ancient Greek stories first recorded thousands of years ago by the poet Homer. At the time, most scholars thought Troy would never be found. Schliemann, on the other hand, was convinced that Homer's epic stories were based on real places and events. About that much, Schliemann was correct. In his rush to find treasure and fame, however, he used dynamite to excavate the site. Countless precious objects were destroyed in the process.

Today, well-trained archaeologists use wire-mesh screens to carefully sift through archaeological sites. Then they use soft brushes to clean every fragment they find, devoted to preserving every piece of useful information. They combine science, art, skill, insight, broad education, and great love for their work. They want to enrich the world, not themselves. These days, looters, not untrained archaeologists, are the main threat to many of the world's most precious archaeological sites.

As you read these articles, all adapted from *National Geographic* and the National Geographic website, notice how much joy archaeologists get from the work they do. It is dirty, uncomfortable, even dangerous. But as you read about their work, maybe you will be inspired to devote yourself to the important job of preserving our shared human past. There is real thrill in finding objects last touched by people thousands of years ago. You can't help but feel a connection with your cousins from the distant past. And by helping the world to understand our common heritage, you may help to bring the world a little closer together.

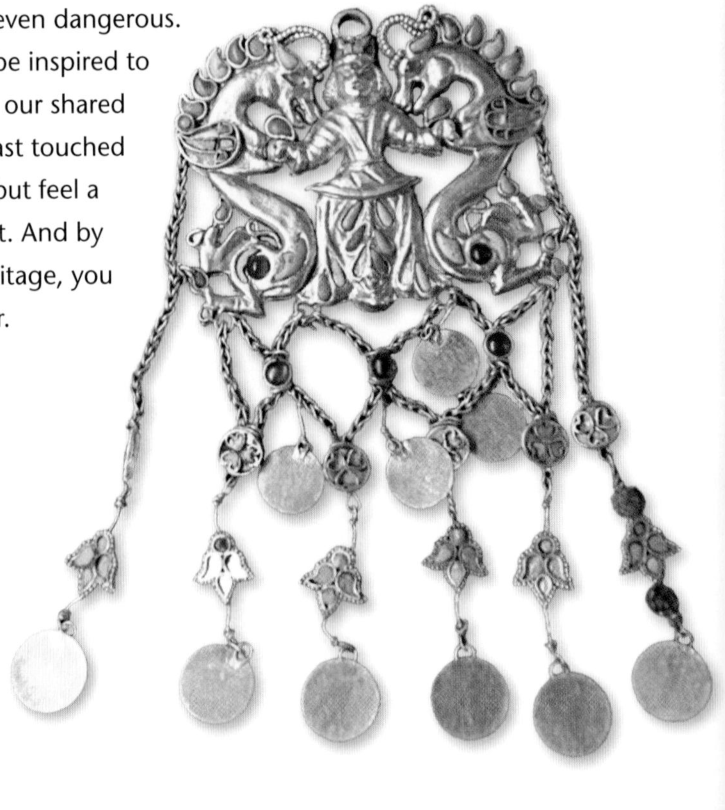

AMAZING FIND
This golden pendant is part of a large treasure found in tombs at the archaeological site Tillya Tepe in Afghanistan.

NATIONAL GEOGRAPHIC

EXPLORER'S JOURNAL

with Fredrik Hiebert

Fredrik Hiebert (second from the left) and his associates work on a dig in Turkmenistan, in Asia.

Have you ever wondered what it's like to travel to a distant land and dig for treasure, sort of like Indiana Jones? Read about real-life archaeologist Fredrik Hiebert's job, how he became an archaeologist, and how he made his all-time favorite discovery.

ACCIDENTAL ARCHAEOLOGIST

Fredrik Hiebert is an archaeologist and a National Geographic Fellow. For more than 20 years, he has been fascinated by ancient trade routes that used to connect major centers of early civilizations, such as the Silk Road. The Silk Road was a network of paths between China and Europe on which goods were traded and ideas were spread. To search for evidence of these civilizations, sometimes Heibert's work takes him under water. Recently, he has begun a project under a lake in Central Asia. Members of the team hope to bring to light **artifacts** from this once critical location along the Silk Road, with paths running along its shores.

Unlike many archaeologists, Hiebert did not feel he was born to the profession. He explains: "I thought I was going to be an artist. And I was trained to draw. I love drawing. I drew anything. I drew nature, I drew objects . . . and because of this, I was able to get my first job working on an archaeological **excavation** drawing artifacts, and I guess that's where the [archaeology] bug bit me. And I became really interested in the story behind the artifacts. So slowly I became more interested in the artifacts than I was in doing the drawings, but I have to admit, I still do all the drawings on my own digs."

When Hiebert isn't in the field uncovering artifacts, he may be cataloging and displaying them for the public to view. Heibert is also a **curator** who puts together exhibits for museums and other locations.

The exhibit "Afghanistan: Hidden Treasures from the National Museum, Kabul" was curated by Hiebert. He went to Afghanistan in 2003

to find out if a number of boxes discovered in a bank vault were treasures that were previously thought lost forever. These rediscovered artifacts toured the world stopping in several major museums. (For more on this exhibit, see "Afghanistan's Hidden Treasures," pages 40–45.)

OUTSIDE THE MUSEUM

Hiebert is eager for the public to learn about and see the beautiful artifacts he uncovers. Going beyond the traditional locations, such as museums and schools, he finds ways to ensure as many people as possible have the opportunity to view the results of his work.

"Anything we can do to help bring the past alive is what archaeologists are really interested in doing," Hiebert says. He found one way to expose several people in Singapore, a country in Southeast Asia, to rare treasures from their part of the world.

Hiebert and his team had just completed a small exhibit on the maritime Silk Road in Arabia and Asia. Not many people visit museums in Southeast Asia. However, thousands of people enjoy shopping in malls. So Hiebert created a self-contained exhibit in

WET AND DRY
Left: Fredrik Hiebert dons a wetsuit to search for ruins at the bottom of a lake in Central Asia. Right: Hiebert catalogs gold jewelry from a bank vault in Kabul, Afghanistan.

malls and parking lots, allowing thousands of people to see the remarkable exhibit.

Another, smaller, place Hiebert teaches archaeology is in the home. "Both of my boys have been on archaeological digs with me, and with me and my wife who's also an archaeologist. And they're not really that interested in the archaeology," he explains. "I guess if you've grown up with it, it doesn't seem all that exotic or different. But they really do love what we do. They love seeing us at work with the excavations, and they know a lot more about looking at the ground sometimes than I do. So I have to ask them questions sometimes."

Hiebert extends his role as educator by teaming up with Lucasfilm, the film studio of George Lucas, who produced the Indiana Jones movies. Together they created the exhibit "Indiana Jones and the Adventure of Archaeology." The story of the fictional archaeologist Indiana Jones is incorporated into the exhibit which teaches visitors about the world of archaeology. Props and video clips from the movie, provided by Lucasfilm Archives, are weaved together with actual artifacts, such as gold jewelry from the Royal Cemetery at Ur, in ancient Mesopotamia and beautifully decorated bowls from Nazca, Peru. National Geographic and the University of Pennsylvania Museum of Archaeology and Anthropology provided the treasures on display. Using the adventures of Indiana Jones as a backdrop to explore the tools and methods used by real-life archaeologists, like Fredrik Hiebert, has made this exhibit quite successful.

BEST DISCOVERIES

In his career as an archaeologist, Hiebert has walked across deserts and has dived hundreds of feet beneath the Black Sea looking for evidence of ancient civilizations.

When people ask Hiebert what archaeological discovery gave him the greatest pleasure, however, he recalls one early experience in his career. The find wasn't a hoard of gold or jewels. It wasn't an item of particular beauty or even of great historic importance. But the find had special meaning for Hiebert.

"This goes back some 20 years ago," he explained, "when I was a student and I was excavating a trade site on the coast of Egypt. This is the Red Sea coast. It's one of the most barren coasts in the whole world. Nothing grows there. There's no water, there are no trees. It's kind of amazing that people had ever even built a town there. The reason people had built a town at this particular site was that it's a great trading place. It's a place where ships would come in. But it's so dry that everything's preserved."

Hiebert continues, "So when we excavated there, we found the house of a merchant who had been on the coast waiting for ships to come in. He had warehouses, and there were remains of many of the things that came in and left through the warehouses of his house.

"Well, we were excavating this house, and we finished the excavation, and there was a reed mat in front of the house that was still preserved. This was about a 700-year-old reed mat. I had done drawings of the house, and we had photographed it, and I thought 'Gee, it's a shame to leave this reed mat here on the ground.' So I pulled it up, and then we made a really interesting discovery. Underneath the mat was the house key the merchant had left 700 years ago. He had hidden his key underneath the doormat, thinking he would return one day. And here we found it. And it even had his name written on it."

LAKE ISSYK KUL

Hiebert's most recent expedition brings him back to underwater archaeology. In 2012, he and a National Geographic team set up a base camp on the northern shore of Issyk Kul (ih-SIHK kuhl), one of the highest and deepest lakes in the world. Once part of the **Mongol** Empire, it is now in the Central Asian republic of Kyrgyzstan. Many researchers believe the ruins of a great palace are at the bottom of the lake. The National Geographic team plans to find out whether that is true. At the time this article was written, the investigation of Issyk Kul was ongoing.

Issyk Kul was a critical location along the fabled Silk Road, with routes running along its shores. Nestled in the largest east-west valley in the high Central Asian mountains, Issyk Kul was noted in historical documents as a strategic point that was battled for over the centuries. Countless traders, caravans, and armies traveled along the

UNDERWATER CLUES
Exploring Lake Issyk Kul, Hiebert examines artifacts that might provide clues to a mystery. Does a great palace lie at the bottom of the deep, frigid lake?

VANISHED VILLAGES
Entire lakeside cities have disappeared beneath the waves of Lake Issyk Kul. Hiebert and his team are continuing decades of work by other archaeologists as they study the ruins of these cities.

113-mile-long lake. They left a rich archaeological legacy behind.

In September 2012, Kristin Romey, director of field operations at Lake Issyk Kul, wrote about the project on the National Geographic website. "Last year, a small National Geographic team conducted a visual and remote sensing survey of the site," she wrote.

The results were encouraging. The team went ahead with the next step of the project. They set up camp near the lake, according to Romey, "armed with a toolkit of high-tech remote sensing equipment," along with their diving and underwater excavation gear. Then they prepared to search.

Hiebert, Romey, and the rest of the team were not the first to take an interest in Issyk Kul, which means "hot lake" in Kyrgyz, the official language of the republic of Kyrgyzstan. As early as the 1860s, it drew attention from researchers for the remains that lie beneath its stunning blue waters. Issyk Kul was one of the earliest sites for underwater archaeological research in Central Asia. It's an endorheic lake (meaning that it has no outlet) with abundant underwater springs, and the water level has risen and fallen dramatically over the centuries. Rising water levels have often flooded settlements, buildings, and even entire cities.

In 1927 the archaeologist P. P. Ivanov carefully studied the underwater ruins and created a map of what he found. He wanted to give future researchers a head start on their work. Unfortunately, his map was never published and only came to light in 1957.

Then in 1959, Dmitri Vinnick of the Kyrgyz Institute of History turned his attention to Issyk Kul. He is the first archaeologist to begin a systematic survey of the site. He reported finding regular walls made of brick, wooden beams, and blue-glazed tiles.

Since 1985, Professor Vladimir Ploskikh of the Kyrgyz Academy of Sciences has been conducting underwater surveys and excavations. In 2010 the National Geographic team began partnering with him. According to Kristin Romey, the main goal is "to finally resolve the question of whether there is truly a legacy of one of the world's most legendary conquerors beneath its waters."

The Mongol leader she is referring to is Tamerlane, also known as Timur, who lived from 1336 to 1405. In the Middle Ages, the region around the lake was hotly contested by two lines of descendants from the great Mongol ruler Genghis Khan: **nomadic** Eastern Mongols and the city-dwelling Western Mongols. The legendary Western Mongol leader Tamerlane was said to have battled for the lake region in the early 1400s, and there are medieval accounts of a palace built by the conqueror on the northern shore of Issyk Kul.

The existence of such a building would be of major importance in helping historians to trace the expansion of Tamerlane's empire. But a more intriguing possibility exists. Could it be that the building was constructed in the magnificent style of Tamerlane's other state buildings? Such a palace would be an amazing find. The question has yet to be answered, but this mind-boggling possibility helps to keep the National Geographic team focused and enthusiastic.

REAL TREASURES

Archaeology has already taken Fredrik Hiebert to places he never dreamed he would see to do things he never dreamed he would do. He loves his job so much he almost forgets it is a job. "Actually, archaeology is a passion," he says of his work. "What we really like, what archaeologists really like to do is keep thinking about new digs, what else we might find, and how we might answer those questions that seem almost impossible to answer."

Though Heibert has discovered priceless cultural treasures and may discover even more in the future, it is his search for knowledge that is most exciting.

THINK ABOUT IT!

1 **Evaluate** Do you think it is important for archaeologists like Fredrik Hiebert to exhibit their work for the public? Why or why not?

2 **Make Generalizations** What qualities does a person need to be a successful archaeologist like Fredrik Hiebert?

3 **Describe Geographic Information** How is it possible that the ruins of a large building could be at the bottom of Lake Issyk Kul?

BACKGROUND & VOCABULARY

artifact *n.* (AHR-tih-fakt) a human-made object from a particular period of time

curator *n.* (KYUR-ay-tur) a person who organizes and manages museum exhibits

excavation *n.* (ehks-kuh-VAY-shuhn) the act or process of digging to uncover buried items

Mongol *adj.* (MAHN-guhl) referring to the empire that spread from present-day Mongolia to encompass most of Asia and part of Europe in the 13th and 14th centuries

nomadic *adj.* (noh-MAD-ihk) having no fixed residence; moving from place to place

The Birth of Religion: Göbekli Tepe

Adapted from "The Birth of Religion," by Charles C. Mann, in *National Geographic*, June 2011

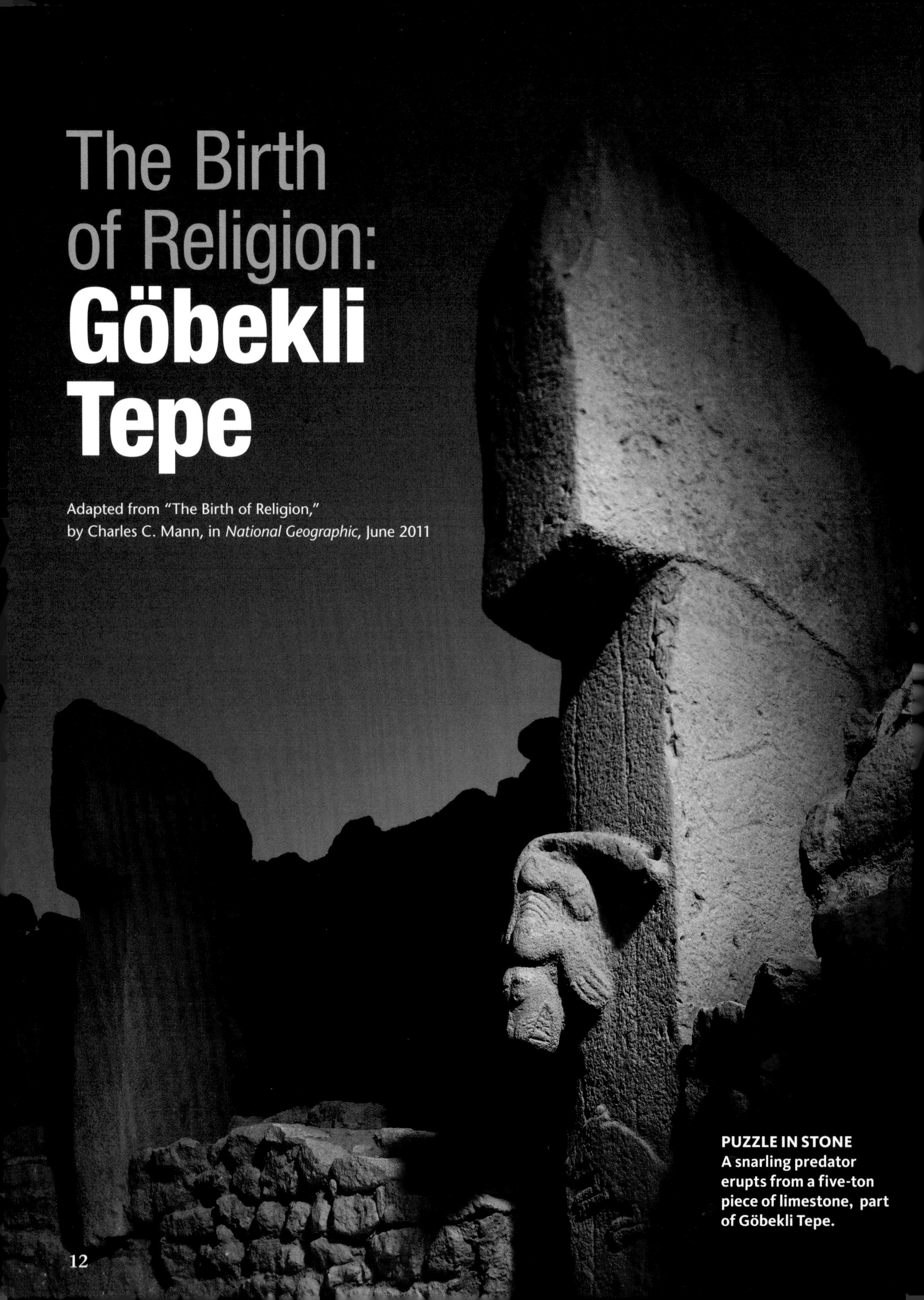

PUZZLE IN STONE
A snarling predator erupts from a five-ton piece of limestone, part of Göbekli Tepe.

Archaeologists assumed agriculture gave rise to cities—and later to writing, art, and religion. Now the world's oldest temple suggests the urge to worship sparked civilization.

MYSTERY AND WONDER

Every now and then a busload of tourists makes the slow ride up a bumpy road to a ridge in southern Turkey. The visitors flood out and climb a steep hill. When they reach the top, their mouths fall open in amazement.

Before them are rings of huge pillars, one next to the other. The site is known as Göbekli Tepe (pronounced guh-behk-LEE TEH-peh). It consists of smooth limestone pillars carved with the images of gazelles, snakes, scorpions, and wild boars. It was built 11,600 years ago—7,000 years before the first pyramids in Egypt. In fact, Göbekli Tepe is the oldest known monumental structure in the world.

When Göbekli Tepe was built, most humans lived in small groups of **foragers**. Yet somehow the temple's builders managed to cut, shape, and transport 16-ton stones without the use of wheels or animal power. Approached from below, Göbekli Tepe's pillars must have looked like spirits from another world.

Archaeologists are still excavating Göbekli Tepe and debating its meaning. It is one of several recent findings that challenge earlier ideas about humanity's past. Twenty years ago the favored theory of the origin of civilization was called the Neolithic Revolution. The theory held that foragers had to first develop agriculture and start moving into small villages. Then villages could grow into cities and civilization could emerge. But new discoveries have forced archaeologists to reconsider the theory.

The **Neolithic Revolution** was believed to have happened first in **Mesopotamia**. The cause was the gradual warming that followed the Ice Age, which let people cultivate plants and herd animals in abundance. New research, however, suggests that the Neolithic Revolution actually occurred across a huge area over thousands of years. And it may not have been driven by climate change.

Archaeologists had surveyed Göbekli Tepe in the 1960s and found little of interest there. In 1994 Klaus Schmidt, now with the German Archaeological Institute, wanted to see it for himself. "Within minutes of getting there," Schmidt says, he realized that he was at a place where hundreds of people had worked in the distant past. He started digging at the site the following year.

Inches below the surface Schmidt's team struck an elaborately carved stone. Then another, and another—a ring of pillars. They now believe there are at least 20 rings buried at Göbekli Tepe.

The pillars were big—as tall as 18 feet. They were covered in carvings of animals, each in a different style. Other parts of the hill were littered with numerous **flint** tools, even though the stone had to be carried to Göbekli Tepe from miles away.

The pillars are all shaped like giant capital Ts and stand about six feet apart. In the middle of each ring are two taller pillars. The outer stones face the center of the circle, as at "a meeting or dance," Schmidt says. He thinks the configuration could represent a religious ritual.

As work continues at Göbekli Tepe, puzzles remain. For some unknown reason, the pillars were buried and replaced with new stones every few decades. Then the whole area was filled in with debris, and an entirely new circle was built inside the first. Surprisingly, the Göbekli Tepe builders got steadily worse at their job. Over time, the pillars became smaller and simpler. The effort seems to have stopped altogether by 8200 B.C.

It must have taken hundreds of workers to erect the pillars, but the nearest water source was about three miles away. Workers would have needed homes, but no signs of houses or cooking fires have been found. To judge by the many gazelle and **auroch** bones found at the site, the workers seem to have been fed with shipments of game brought from faraway hunts.

BUILDING GÖBEKLI TEPE
This illustration suggests how temple builders brought rough stones from nearby quarries, then shaped and carved them before setting them upright. The pillars are incorporated into circular stone walls, creating rooms.

A NEW THEORY OF CIVILIZATION

To Schmidt, discovering that foragers had constructed Göbekli Tepe was like learning that someone had built a 747 airplane in a basement. The feat is amazing, but it is still not clear how it was done or what it means. "In 10 or 15 years," Schmidt predicts, "Göbekli Tepe will be more famous than Stonehenge. And for good reason."

Hovering over Göbekli Tepe is the ghost of V. Gordon Childe, one of the most influential archaeologists of the past century. Childe's special talent was weaving together disconnected facts into coherent theories. His most famous theory is the concept of the Neolithic Revolution, proposed in the 1920s.

According to Childe, humans arose 200,000 years ago, living in small groups of wandering foragers. In a flash of inspiration, Mesopotamians turned from foraging to agriculture. To adopt farming, people had to stop wandering and move into permanent villages, where they developed new tools. In Childe's view, the Neolithic Revolution was the biggest thing since "the mastery of fire."

The key event was the development of agriculture. For thousands of years humans had foraged for wild grain, but farming allowed people to grow as much grain as they needed. Population soared. "It was only after the revolution—but immediately thereafter—that our species really began to multiply at all fast," Childe wrote. In the growing cities, technical innovations multiplied and civilization was able to flourish.

In Childe's day it was thought that the earliest cities in Mesopotamia represented the beginning of civilization. But later, settlements dating as far back as 13,000 B.C. were discovered near the eastern Mediterranean coast. Known as Natufian villages, they appeared as the Ice Age was ending, during a 2,000-year-long warm and wet period.

The discovery of the Natufians was the first challenge to Childe's Neolithic Revolution. Childe had said there was no civilization without farming, yet the Natufians lived in permanent villages but didn't farm.

The Natufian evidence called for a new theory of farming's origins. Some suggested that after the warm, wet period ended, the Natufians had to adapt to a much cooler, drier climate. It was only then that they developed agriculture, to ensure a more reliable food supply.

As the debate over civilization's origin continued, Schmidt was making progress at Göbekli Tepe. What he found would force many researchers to reassess their ideas yet again.

Anthropologists have assumed that organized religion arose only after foragers became farmers and developed large societies. Compared to foraging, village life has more complex goals—storing grain and maintaining permanent homes. Success would be more likely if villagers were committed to working together toward common goals. Organized religion arose, in this view, only when communities needed a common vision of how the world works. Communities united in a common world view were more likely to cooperate.

To Schmidt, Göbekli Tepe suggests this theory is wrong. The existence of a massive temple built by foragers shows that organized religion could have come before agriculture. It suggests that the human impulse to gather for sacred rituals arose as humans shifted from seeing themselves as part of the natural world to seeking mastery over it.

Schmidt thinks that foragers living near Göbekli Tepe created the temple as a holy place to gather and meet. Some social organization would be required to build it. One imagines chanting and drumming, the animals on the great pillars seeming to move in flickering torchlight.

Over time, Schmidt believes, the need to acquire sufficient food for those who visited Göbekli Tepe may have led to the development of farms. Indeed, scientists now believe that a center of agriculture arose in southern Turkey about the time the temple was thriving. In other words, the development of agriculture may have been the result of a deep human need to see spectacles.

Not everyone agrees with Schmidt. More and more, archaeologists studying the origins of civilization distrust attempts to single out one primary trigger. Maybe civilization was arrived at by different means in different places.

Schmidt believes his colleagues have been as slow to appreciate Göbekli Tepe as he has been to excavate it. The summer of 2011 marked his 17th year at the site, and yet less than a tenth of the 22-acre site had been explored.

Schmidt admits that further research may change his view of the site's importance. "We come up with two new mysteries for every one that we solve," he says. Still, he has already drawn some conclusions. "Twenty years ago everyone believed civilization was driven by ecological forces," Schmidt says. "I think what we are learning is that civilization is a product of the human mind."

THINK ABOUT IT!

1 **Summarize** Describe the importance of the development of agriculture in the theory of the Neolithic Revolution.

2 **Analyze Cause and Effect** What role might climate change have played in the development of civilization?

3 **Compare and Contrast** According to Karl Schmidt, what does the discovery of Göbekli Tepe suggest about the origin of religion? How does this differ from previous theories of the origin of religion?

BACKGROUND & VOCABULARY

anthropologist *n.* (an-thruh-PAH-luh-jihst) a scientist who studies the history and development of human beings

auroch *n.* (AWR-ahk) an extinct wild ox that prehistoric people hunted in Europe

flint *n.* (FLIHNT) a type of stone that can be broken into thin pieces with sharp edges, like a knife

forager *n.* (FAW-ruh-jur) a person who collects food instead of growing it

Mesopotamia *n.* (MEH-suh-puh-TAY-mee-ah) the area in southern Iraq between the Tigris and Euphrates rivers

Neolithic Revolution *n.* (nee-aw-LIH-thihk reh-veh-LOO-shun) a theory about the transition of humans from hunters and gatherers to a society of farmers

The Pyramid Builders

BY VIRGINIA MORELL

Adapted from "The Pyramid Builders," by Virginia Morell, in *National Geographic*, November 2001

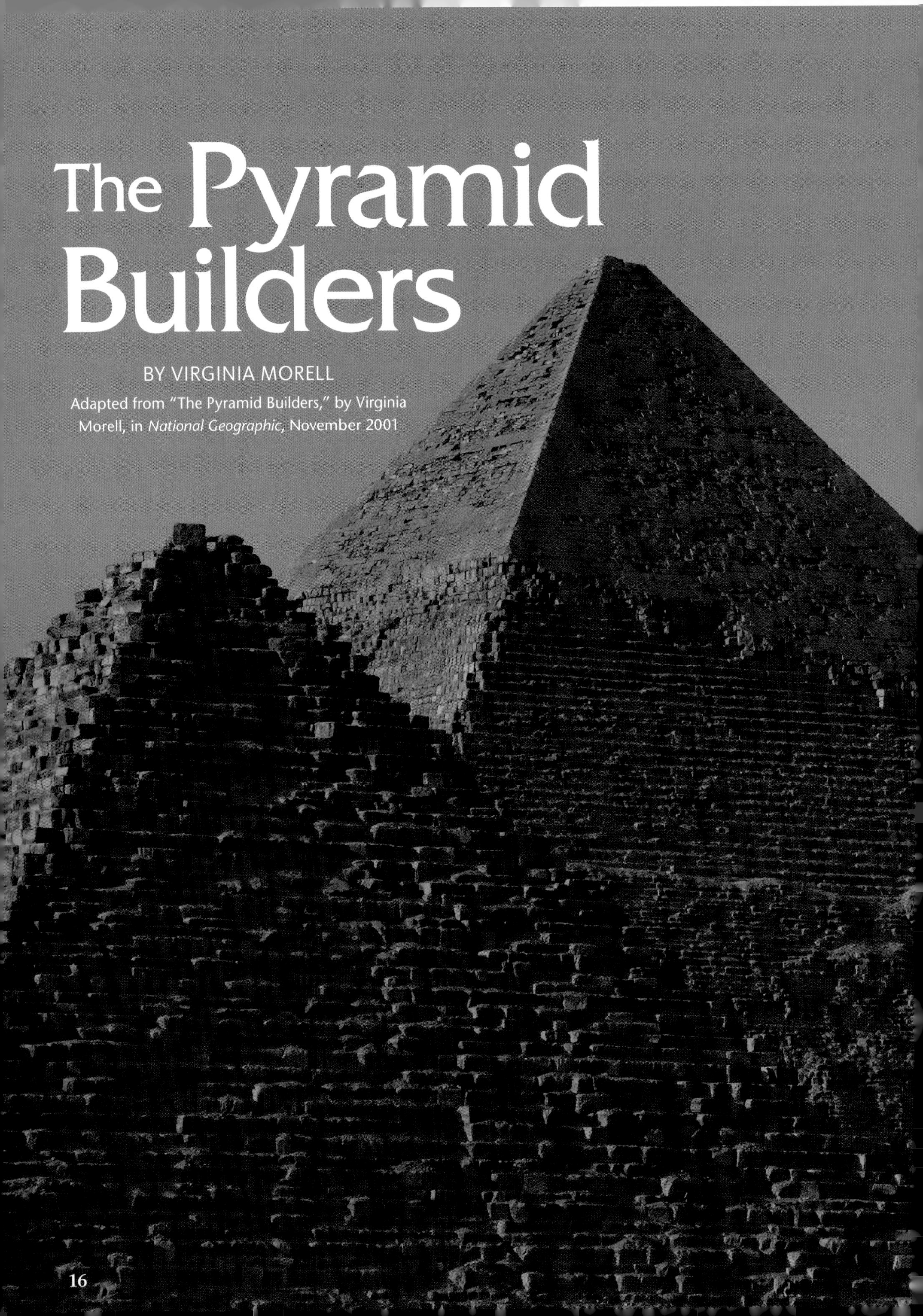

Who built the great pyramids at Giza more than 4,000 years ago? Writer Virginia Morell joined Egyptologist Zahi Hawass in his quest to understand the pyramid builders.

EXCAVATIONS NEAR GIZA

The pyramids were built of stone blocks ranging from less than one ton to more than 40 tons. All were cut, moved, and set in place by human hands. The ancient Egyptians used neither complex machines nor animals for any of this labor. And after they completed the core of a pyramid, they covered it with stones fitted together and polished until the pyramids gleamed like jewels in the sun.

On a sand-covered hill outside Cairo, Egypt, near the three great pyramids at Giza, Egyptologist [someone who studies ancient Egyptian culture and artifacts] Zahi Hawass picks a path among small tombs built of mud and stone. Some of the graves are shaped like beehives. Others are structures carved into the rocky cliffs. Some are built from stone blocks, decorated with carvings. Still others are little more than small lumps of earth, studded with broken chunks of stone.

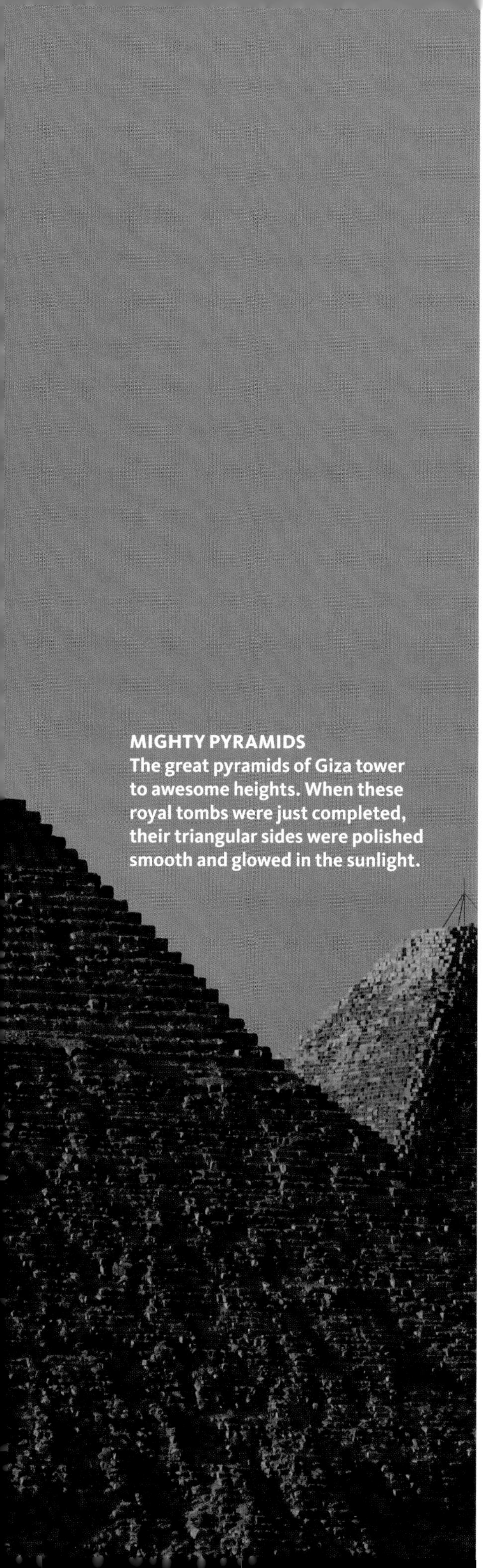

MIGHTY PYRAMIDS
The great pyramids of Giza tower to awesome heights. When these royal tombs were just completed, their triangular sides were polished smooth and glowed in the sunlight.

"It's something I wondered about for years," Hawass tells me, taking a seat on a nearby rock while members of his crew dig carefully into the top of one of the cemetery's tombs. "Many times when I looked at the pyramids, I would ask myself about the workers who built them. Where were they buried? Who were the men and women behind this great enterprise? Because of these graves, we have some clues."

Hawass's discovery of this cemetery in 1990, along with archaeologist Mark Lehner's nearby excavations of an ancient city, confirms what Egyptologists had suspected. Ordinary Egyptian citizens built the three pyramids. Some worked as forced labor for periods of time, others as full-time employees. Hawass and Lehner estimate that the feat—cutting, transporting, and shaping 7 million cubic yards of stone—was accomplished by only 10,000 workers. Each pyramid complex was started when a **pharaoh** assumed the throne and stopped when he died. Thus the Giza monuments, which were built during the reigns of kings Khufu, Khafre, and Menkaure, required some 80 years to build.

"Many times when I looked at the pyramids, I would ask myself about the workers who built them. Where were they buried? Who were the men and women behind this great enterprise?"

—ZAHI HAWASS

A CITY OF EFFICIENT WORKERS

"They were proud of their work, yes," says Hawass when I comment on the evident care of the pyramid builders. "It's because they were not *just* building the tomb of their king. They were building Egypt. It was a national project, and everyone was a participant."

"Imagine working under the hot Egyptian sun with a stone pick or copper chisel to cut these blocks of stone and then pushing and pulling them to make a pyramid. What motivated them? The most we can say . . . is that they were deeply religious and believed that by building the tomb for their king, they were assuring his rebirth as well as their own and that of Egypt overall," Lehner suggests. Even the poorest workers were buried with something for the afterlife. It might be as simple as a knife to cut meat or a clay jar filled with a favorite drink.

To build such monumental structures, the Egyptians needed a highly organized workforce. From tomb **inscriptions** and from laborers' instructions on walls, researchers can now draw something close to an organization chart for the ancient workers. "Every project like a pyramid had a crew of workers," explains Ann Roth, an Egyptologist who has studied the groups of workers in detail. "And each group was responsible for one part of the pyramid complex. There was one group for building the interior granite roofs and separate groups for raising the chamber walls." Managers directed teams of workers and shipments of supplies coming in from all over Egypt.

"They had to be very organized," says Lehner, "to build these things as quickly as they did." He notes that to construct a pyramid in 20 years' time, the workers had to set a stone in place every two minutes.

To keep the workforce moving at top speed, a highly developed support force was also needed, notes Lehner. "You have to have a place to feed and house all these workers and the . . . bakers, brewers, and butchers who support them." In other words, you need a city. And Lehner thinks he has found at least part of that city.

On a wide, sandy plain below Hawass's cemetery, Lehner and his crew have excavated carefully laid out paved streets and well-designed buildings. Inside, the buildings are divided into small rooms and linked by hallways. The members of Lehner's team are now excavating the area that he calls South Street.

"It's our third such street here, and it runs parallel to the other two. It was a **gridded** city and quite unusual for its time," says Lehner. Before its discovery some Egyptologists thought that ancient settlements would have looked like expanded villages. Lehner's excavations have proved that idea wrong. The city near Giza was substantial and well organized, with straight streets and areas set aside for work.

Lehner is still unsure about the overall purpose of the city's working area. "Was it here solely to feed the workers?" he asks, leaning down to sweep away the sand from a tiny fish spine. "Or did they use buildings . . . to prepare offerings for the temples?" There are no papyrus texts or wall inscriptions—not even any ancient graffiti—to give an answer. The only written clues come from markings on the tiny scraps of clay that once sealed the mouths of jars and sacks of grain. These markings are like little identifying tags. According to Egyptologist John Nolan, "Sealed goods were the closest thing to money these people had. The sealings established a chain of responsibility. There was the person who put the sealing on and the person with the authority to break it." Nolan has thousands of sealings left to read. Someday one may answer the question of how closely Hawass' cemetery and Lehner's city are connected in time.

ARCHAEOLOGIST AT WORK Inside the pyramid of the ancient king Khufu, Zahi Hawass examines a skeleton in a simple stone coffin.

THE TOMBS OF THE WEALTHY

Most of the graves are those of poor workers. Several, though, mark the resting places of wealthy officials. Some of these are built like miniature versions of royal temples. They are rectangular and made of stone blocks. And they have everything a tomb should have: carved false doors for the person's spirit to exit the tomb, stone offering basins, and inscriptions giving the owner's name and title and the names of his wife and children. Two even have ramps leading up to their doorways, like the long ramps to the three pyramids.

The owners of these two tombs "wanted them to look as much like those of their pharaohs as possible," says Hawass. "This one is the tomb of Weser-Petah, overseer of the officials." It is a simple structure like a narrow but shortened railroad car. Above the false door and on either side of it are carvings showing Weser-Petah in the classic Egyptian profile. Beside and below them are symbols giving his name and title. The carvings are not as elaborate as the tomb inscriptions of the ruling class. However, they still reveal a concern for having a good afterlife.

A few steps away is the tomb of Ni-ankh-Petah, overseer of the king's bakeries and cakes. And uphill from his tomb stands that of Nefer-Theith, overseer of the palace. Other tombs bear such titles as overseer of the rowers, overseer of the side of the pyramid, inspector of the royal gardens, and master of the harbor. So far, Hawass's team has discovered 26 of these titles.

"The titles are those of mid- to high-level managers," notes Hawass. "[They] further demonstrate the tight organization of the ancient Egyptian workforce."

Many upper-class women were buried in the tombs of their husbands. Often they too had their names and titles carved above the false doorways, as did the wife of Petty, inspector of the craftsmen. Her name was Nesy-Sokar. She was a priestess of Hathor, goddess of love and dance. Two women had their own tombs. One, like Nesy-Sokar, was a priestess of Hathor. The other was a priestess of Neith, goddess of war.

SEEN FROM ABOVE
An aerial view of Giza reveals the straight, gridded streets of the pyramid builders' city, at the lower right of the photo.

Like the pharaohs, titled officials—men and women—often had various goods placed in their tombs to help them in the afterlife. These sometimes included small offering plates and drinking cups. They were made of clay and about the size of a child's tea party set. "There was nothing of real value in these tombs," says Hawass, "which is why they were not looted."

Still, the owners worried about protecting their tombs against thieves. In the tomb of Petty and Nesy-Sokar was carved a row of curses. One reads: "As for any person, male or female, who shall do evil against this tomb . . . the crocodile shall be against him upon water, the hippopotamus shall be against him in the water, and the scorpion shall be against him on land."

Some of the tombs contained small statues of their owners. Most of these, such as the statue of Nefer-ef-Nesu, chief of the sculptors, and his wife Nefer-Menkhes, were carved from stone, then painted. The statue shows the couple seated side by side on a bench. She wears a fancy net dress, a beaded necklace, and bracelets. He is dressed in a simple white kilt. They both face forward, with slight smiles. She has her right arm around her husband's shoulder. "It is their ideal, how they want to be in the afterlife," says Tarek El-Awady, an archaeologist and assistant to Hawass. "So they want to look their best and wear the best clothes and jewelry." Indeed, the statue presents an attractive picture of a couple ready for the afterlife that awaits.

WORKERS' HEALTH

For most of the fancy tomb owners, daily life was probably not too difficult. But for the laborers, life was surely hard. "We can see that in their skeletons," says Azza Mohamed Sarry El-Din, who is studying the skeletal remains from the cemetery. "I've looked at 175 skeletons so far, about half men, half women, and nearly all of them suffered from **arthritis**. Their **lumbar vertebrae** are badly compressed, as you would expect for a manual workforce. I expected to see that, but I was surprised to see this kind of arthritis in the women too." The condition of the women's bones suggests to Sarry El-Din that they were moving heavy loads. "There is more damage to their bones than you would expect from simply doing household chores."

Some of the skeletons also show that the workers may not have had the best diet. Sarry El-Din's analysis suggests that some individuals didn't have enough iron in their diets and that most of the laborers ate very little meat. But the workers did have good medical care. One worker suffered a badly injured arm, which a doctor **amputated** below the elbow. The operation healed as well as a similar amputation performed on the leg of an official.

"Both men recovered and lived for many years after their accidents," says Sarry El-Din. "Someone was taking care of these laborers. Workers who are pushing stones around . . . are going to be hurt. [The] overseers knew this and had a clinic for them."

Despite the availability of medical care, the workers' lives were short. On average a man lived 40 to 45 years, and a woman lived 30 to 35. "The women's lives were shorter, probably because of problems in childbirth," says Sarry El-Din. "But very few people were living what we think of as a long life."

Standing on a hill above his site, Lehner says, "You could look at this as a fairly miserable existence. There would have been hundreds of fires burning to bake the bread, to make the pottery. . . . The air was probably thick with smoke, and there were people moving in long lines to pull the blocks to the pyramid site and people grinding grains, butchering cattle, probably unloading goods in a harbor. . . . It was all hard, hot, sweaty labor." And what did it get you? "It gave you a job, a way of making a living, and it gave you a national purpose. And, for them at least, it gave them life beyond this world."

Postscript: The archaeologists excavating the tombs of the pyramid workers have more recently discovered that the cemetery extends farther north and south. Beside the tomb of the overseer of the workmen lie the remains of his workmen. These tombs confirm that the workers were organized into gangs and that each gang had a name, such as "friends of Khufu," and an overseer.

THINK ABOUT IT!

1 **Categorize** What types of information are archaeologists able to discover from the evidence the ancient Egyptians left?

2 **Form and Support Opinions** Do you think the pyramid workers were treated fairly? Give reasons to support your opinion.

BACKGROUND & VOCABULARY

amputate *v.* (AMP-yoo-tayt) to cut a limb, such as an arm or leg, from the body

arthritis *n.* (arth-RY-tihs) a painful condition affecting the joints of the body, often caused by wear and tear on the joints

gridded *adj.* (GRIHD-uhd) having a regular grid shape, with lines crossing at right angles

inscription *n.* (ihn-SCRIHP-shuhn) something written or engraved as a lasting record; words written or engraved, as on a monument

lumbar vertebrae *n.* (LUHM-bahr VUR-tuh-bray) the bones in the lower spine

pharaoh *n.* (FAIR-oh) the title of the rulers of ancient Egypt

In Rome's

Adapted from "In Rome's Basement," by Paul Bennett, in *National Geographic*, July 2006

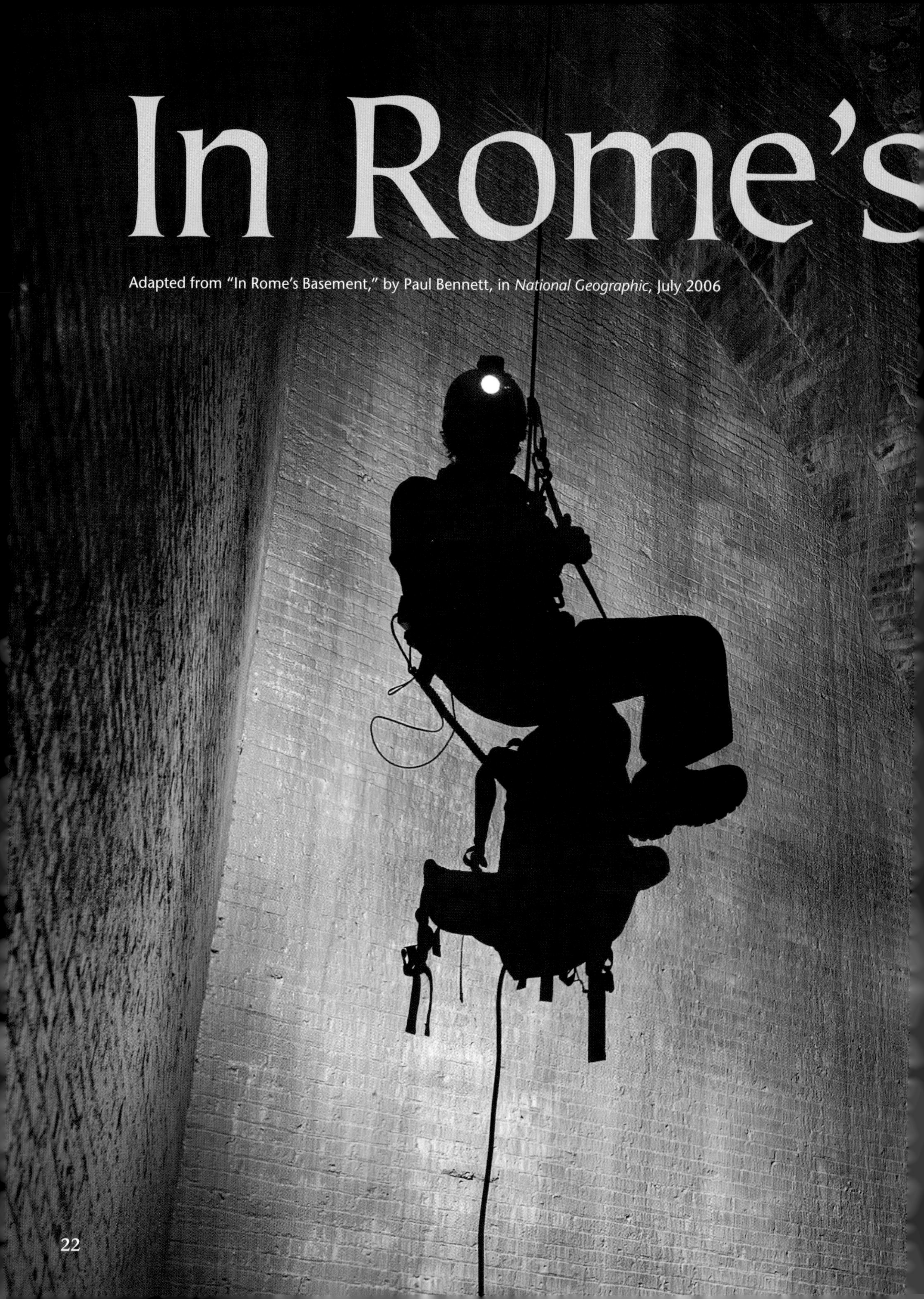

Basement

SECRET MUSEUM
Dangling two stories below a historic Roman hillside, urban explorer Adriano Morabito gazes at a beautifully preserved 2,000-year-old mosaic depicting a grape harvest.

Below the city of Rome lies the world's largest undiscovered museum. Writer Paul Bennett followed the team that walks through sewers that haven't been seen in more than 2,000 years.

INTO THE SEWERS

Luca pushes his head into a dark hole, inhales, and grins. "It doesn't smell so bad in the [sewer] today," he says, dropping himself down underground. Despite his optimism, the blackness emits the sickening aroma you'd expect from a sewer used continuously for 2,500 years. Below in the dark cavern itself, it isn't much better. Luca wades through olive green water, stepping over fragments of temples and building stone washed down over the ages. Signs of modern life float past: cigarette butts, plastic bags, and a baby pacifier. There is also a lot of stringy, gray stuff that looks like toilet paper. This is disturbing, because raw sewage isn't supposed to be flowing through here. Luca points out a broken **amphora**, perhaps 2,000 years old, next to a broken beer bottle, perhaps a week old. Together, they provide a striking testament to how long people have been throwing their garbage into the gutters of this city.

Luca Antognoli works for a group that Rome's government has commissioned to explore its underground spaces. His job takes him through a maze of temples, roads, houses, and **aqueducts** buried since the fall of the Roman Empire. According to tradition, the Cloaca Maxima (or "great drain") was built in the sixth century B.C. That would make it one of the city's oldest—if not the oldest—surviving structures. So it is surprising to learn that the cloaca has never been fully explored and mapped.

In real life Luca Antognoli is a surgeon, and he has warned us to be careful not to expose our skin to the polluted water. He takes his own advice, covering every inch of his body. He wears gloves, boots, mask, and hooded wind suit, all sealed with duct tape. He motions sharply at a pipe spewing a brown liquid into the cavern. As toxic droplets fill the air, members of the group hurry to fit their masks tightly over their faces.

He points out other pipes, some dumping clean water from underground springs, some releasing dirty water. At one point, we pass through a dangerous sloping area covered with sludge. Beyond, a deep hole forces everyone to inch along an unseen ledge in chest-high, scum-covered water.

The adventure comes to a halt at a pile of rubble. The bones, pottery sherds, and caked mud nearly fill the entire space of the sewer, which clearly reaches into the darkness beyond—one wonders how far.

Luca's group plans to send a remote-controlled robot to probe beyond the barrier. He expects to confirm that the great drain extends nearly a mile to the northeast. Who knows what treasures lie along the way, he says. Archaeologists had recently pulled a colossal head of Emperor Constantine from a sewer just like this. Some now believe Constantine, the first Christian emperor, may have been the victim of *damnatio memoriae*, the ancient Roman practice of obliterating the memory of hated emperors.

Rome ruled an empire from the edge of Scotland to Baghdad, shaping much of Western history. For Luca Antognoli, underground spaces like the Cloaca Maxima offer clues about how the city grew.

BURIED HISTORY

The cloaca, originally an open drain, was intentionally buried during the time of the Roman Republic (509–27 B.C.). But most of what's under Rome is there by accident, buried by centuries of urban growth.

"Rome has been rising for 3,000 years," says Darius Arya, an archaeologist and director of the American Institute for Roman Culture. Much of Rome is situated in a floodplain at a bend of the Tiber River. Although the Romans put up levees, or earthen walls to hold back the water, the city

COLLIDING WORLDS
Passersby on the busy streets of modern Rome take a moment to peer into a once-buried ancient stadium built around A.D. 86.

still flooded periodically. So they built upward, laying new structures and streets on top of older ones. "It was cost-effective, and it worked," Arya says. "We see the Romans jacking their city up two meters at a time, raising themselves above the water but also burying their past."

Today the city sits on layers of history 45 feet deep in places. You can dig a hole anywhere within the 12-mile ring of walls that once enclosed the ancient city and find something interesting. But very little of this buried city has been excavated.

"I don't imagine more than ten percent has been documented," says archaeologist Robert Coates-Stevens. For the past decade he has been trying to map the **topography** of ancient Rome. The Roman Forum, a large open area and public meeting place, was dug out during the 1800s, but most ancient structures remain trapped under modern streets and office buildings. "It's a heady feeling," Coates-Stevens says, "to think that all this still lies beneath our feet awaiting discovery."

In the 1920s and 1930s, Italy's dictator Benito Mussolini was seized with this kind of excitement. He destroyed sections of Rome's historic center, where medieval and Renaissance houses stood, to reveal the layers below. He was especially interested in anything dating back to the time of Emperor Augustus, the founder of the Roman Empire. (Mussolini liked to compare himself to Augustus.)

By the 1980s this big-hole approach had fallen out of favor. It was proving costly to protect the ruins Mussolini had exposed. Curiosity about Rome is eternal, however, and so the strategy changed. Archaeologists are now exploring ancient spaces from below the city, leaving the surface undisturbed.

Cristiano Ranieri pulls a dry suit over his head and fixes a full-face respirator in place. Above, the hum of traffic bounces off the stone and brick surfaces of the **Colosseum**. Down here the sound is muffled. Ranieri is down in the maze of passages where gladiators would have waited. He becomes visibly excited as he describes scuba diving beneath the Colosseum. He explains that this space, inside the 40-foot-deep foundation that holds up the rest of the structure, isn't even the bottom. He removes a steel plate from the floor to reveal a still body of dark gray water several yards below. This is the underbelly of the underbelly of the Colosseum.

HIDDEN TOMB
Skulls and bones of monks, some of whom died five centuries ago, adorn a crypt beneath the church of Santa Maria della Concezione.

Ranieri is scouting a new access point into the drain system for a future measuring project. In particular, he wants to know whether he can fit a full underwater lighting rig through this hole. Otherwise, he will need to use portable flashlights. A well-lit swim below the Colosseum could change history.

Until three years ago only a quarter of the pipes running below the Colosseum had been explored. These simple drains were designed to whisk away storm water. They were constructed in the late first century A.D., when the Roman emperors were building the Colosseum. Some ancient writers claimed the building was deliberately flooded so that ships could conduct mock battles before spectators. But there was no evidence of the large waterworks needed to bring in that much water.

Then in 2003, Ranieri made a startling discovery. Below the simple drains (and predating the Colosseum) he found larger pipes. They were built by Emperor Nero to fill an artificial lake in his gardens. The pipes had been reused by the architects of the Colosseum, most likely to

bring water in and out. For the first few years of its history, at least, it was possible to flood the Colosseum to entertain the people.

ACCIDENTAL DISCOVERIES

Most of Rome's hidden secrets are revealed by chance, not planned expeditions. Sometimes, street workers suddenly find they are digging into a hollow underground space. Then there is the discovery made on the Oppian Hill in 2004. After a period of intense rain, a hole opened near a tree, exposing several underground rooms.

Marco Placidi, a colleague of Luca Antognoli, was called in. Using ropes and harnesses, Placidi lowered himself into a dark, 40-foot-high room. Built sometime between A.D. 65 and 109, it is one of the best preserved features from the Roman world. But for Placidi, the heart-thumping moment came halfway down, when he aimed his headlamp at the wall. On it was a mosaic, in perfect condition, showing a group of men harvesting and stamping grapes. It is some ten feet long and made of tiny, brightly colored bits of marble and other stone. "When I dropped down into this hole, I never imagined I'd see something like this," Placidi says. "It was an immense joy."

To an outsider, the randomness of such discoveries is shocking. But for Romans, it's a common experience. Every year, the city authorizes 13,000 requests for building permits, and each one needs archaeological evaluation. Construction of roads and sewers in Rome's suburbs is years behind schedule because of the number of discoveries that have to be checked out before building can proceed.

The city of Rome has been trying hard to extend a sewer to the Appian area in the southeast for the past three years. But it has made little progress, according to Davide Mancini and Sergio Fontana. The two men run a group of archaeology graduate students called Parsifal, which helps the city monitor the work of construction crews. Parsifal oversees up to 20 worksites at a time. They look out for artifacts, report back to the government, and halt work when necessary. Traditional archaeology is painstakingly slow, but Parsifal's experts must work fast. They must be able to spot precious objects and assess their value in the seconds before the shovel digs in.

On a typical day, a backhoe has to stop four times every half hour. A harried graduate student jumps into the muddy pit and tosses up treasure. It might be a lamp, several plates and bowls, or small terra-cotta sculptures. Often objects date from the third or fourth century B.C.

"This zone is a mess," Davide says. He explains that work began here in 2003, expecting the project would take a few months. But completion is still nowhere in sight.

Interruptions such as these cannot be planned for in advance. It is impossible to know what the underground has in store. Beyond that, the length of any delay depends on the value assigned to what is found. Some things, like amphorae sherds, can be quickly dismissed. Others, like buildings, may need to be sketched and measured. Occasionally, the Italian state may require that a unique find be made accessible to the public.

STILL WORKING

Marco Placidi and Adriano Morabito get very quiet and serious when they slide into their dry suits and descend the spiral staircase called La Chiocciola ("snail shell") in central Rome. To them, this is sacred space. The bottom step drops off into the Aqua Virgo, an underground aqueduct carved through solid rock in 19 B.C. It travels more than ten miles to bring the most constant pure water supply Romans have ever enjoyed. The aqueduct is still in use, feeding several fountains including the beautiful Trevi Fountain—a tourist favorite.

The city of Rome surveyed the Aqua Virgo for its water utility several years ago. They used lasers and compasses, occasionally popping to the surface for a GPS reality check. This day the group has returned to double-check earlier work.

The water, at cheek level, comes directly from a spring and is pretty cold. The walls of the Aqua Virgo are cut from solid stone and remarkably regular, like the blocks of the Cloaca Maxima. But the two spaces couldn't be more different. One brings pure, life-giving water. The other takes away foul sewage. These two systems formed part of the circulatory system that kept ancient Rome alive and well.

The group presses on toward the Trevi Fountain. Nick De Pace, who is studying Rome's underground structures, points out the curved lines where excavators scratched their way through the solid rock 2,000 years ago. He describes a work crew using hand tools to chisel, by torchlight, a smooth, sloping conduit. To modern eyes, it looks as if it had been made by machine. For him, Rome's aqueducts and sewers symbolize the can-do spirit of Roman civilization. "Nobody thinks the sewers are that important," he says. "But for me they explain how and why Rome existed."

The exploring party comes to a concrete wall where water is diverted into a modern pipe. Might the pipe lead to a new branch veering off to feed some buried ancient building whose discovery would bring ancient Rome into sharper focus?

"Rome is the biggest open-air museum in the world," says Darius Arya. "There's so much to explore. I find it funny that people talk about diving to the bottom of the sea or climbing faraway peaks. Here's Rome, where we still don't know what's underneath."

THINK ABOUT IT!

1 **Make Inferences** What might happen if the city of Rome allowed residents to dig on their property without official supervision?

2 **Identify Problems and Solutions** Why is it difficult to explore Rome's underground structures? How do explorers overcome these difficulties?

BACKGROUND & VOCABULARY

amphora *n.* (am-FOR-uh) an oval-shaped container with two handles used to store liquids such as wine or olive oil

aqueduct *n.* (AK-wuh-duhkt) a human-built channel for carrying flowing water

Colosseum *n.* (kahl-uh-SEE-uhm) The Colosseum is a large arena built in Rome during the first century. Romans packed the Colosseum to see fights between gladiators, wild animal hunts, dramas, and other spectacles.

topography *n.* (tuh-PAH-gruh-fee) the shape of the land, including natural and human-made features

THE GOLDEN CHIEFS OF PANAMA

Adapted from "The Golden Chiefs of Panama," by A. R. Williams, in *National Geographic*, January 2012

HUMAN OR ANIMAL?
This golden pendant, found in a tomb in Panama, depicts a chief with pelican legs and a feathered headdress.

GOLDEN WARRIORS

In a grassy, sun-dried field in central Panama, gold was coming out of the ground so fast that archaeologist Julia Mayo wanted to yell, Stop, stop! For years she had been waiting for this moment, but now she was overwhelmed.

Mayo was determined to find new evidence of the ancient society she had been studying for years. Mayo and her team began **geophysical** surveys in 2005 at a site known as El Caño, named for a waterfall on one of the area's many rivers. The results identified a circle of long-forgotten graves. By 2010 she and her team had dug a pit 16 feet deep and discovered the remains of a warrior chieftain adorned in gold. The gold items included two embossed breastplates, four arm cuffs, and a bracelet of bells. There were also thousands of golden beads. Some were as plump as olives, and some were tiny spheres. Other beads, shaped like tubes, traced a zigzag pattern on a lower leg. That alone would be the find of a lifetime, but it was just the beginning.

The team returned in the winter 2011 dry season and unearthed a second burial as rich as the first. It was the grave of another supreme chief. This warrior had been buried with two gold breastplates in front, two in back, four arm cuffs, and a brilliant emerald. Near him lay a baby adorned the same way, most likely his son. Beneath them stretched a layer of tangled human skeletons, possibly sacrificed slaves or war captives. Tests dated the burials to about A.D. 900. At that time the Maya civilization, 800 miles to the northwest, was beginning to decline.

Mayo barely had time to catalog the new finds before her team uncovered still more gold. Shining from the walls of the pit, the items marked the edges of four more tombs. As she looked over the scene, she was simply amazed. "I was just speechless—fascinated, but also worried," she remembers.

By that time, the rainy season had already begun, and a nearby river threatened to flood the site. She was now in a race to retrieve all the treasure before it was under water. Also, she knew looters were sure to come if news of the discoveries got out. She swore her team to silence and prayed for clear skies.

DIGGING IN PANAMA

This wasn't the first time that an archaeological gold mine had been found in Panama. At Sitio Conte, less than two miles from where Mayo was working, one of the Western Hemisphere's greatest collections of artifacts was found. In the early 1900s a rain-swollen river sliced into a cattle pasture. Golden breastplates and other items washed out of tombs and down the riverbank.

News of the ancient cemetery spread, and soon a team of archaeologists set off on the long voyage by ship from New York to Panama City. From there, they travelled by horse, oxcart, and dugout canoe to get to Sitio Conte. For four years they dug, often in brutal heat. They opened almost 100 tombs, many holding multiple bodies adorned in gold. They also found other works by skilled artisans: painted **ceramics**, carved whale bones decorated with gold, and necklaces of sharks' teeth.

In 1937 Harvard archaeologist Samuel Lothrop wrote a report about Sitio Conte. In it he identified the people living in this region as one of the native groups the Spanish met when they invaded Panama in the early 1500s. As the **conquistadors** marched across the isthmus, or narrow strip of land, they kept detailed records. In the Sitio Conte region they noted small, warlike communities battling for control. Warrior chiefs covered themselves in gold to show their rank as they fought each other and the Spanish.

The conquistadors took a fortune in gold for the royal coffers back in Spain as they defeated chief after chief. From one funeral alone they plundered 355 pounds of gold. They even tore jewelry from the bodies of three chiefs who had been mummified after falling in battle.

The Sitio Conte culture is much older than Lothrop thought. Experts now believe the graves of the warrior chiefs date from about the ninth century. The artifacts seemed to match the descriptions left by the conquistadors because some aspects of the culture in the 1500s hadn't changed for many centuries.

By April 1940 the workers at Sitio Conte had found a wealth of artifacts for their museums, and they went home. A few others continued to search Panama's green pastures, with little success. This part of Central America has

BURIAL PIT AT EL CAÑO

Located near Panama's Pacific coast, this tomb held a supreme chief, people sacrificed to serve him for eternity, and containers of food. The pit was open and roofed, perhaps so survivors could visit.

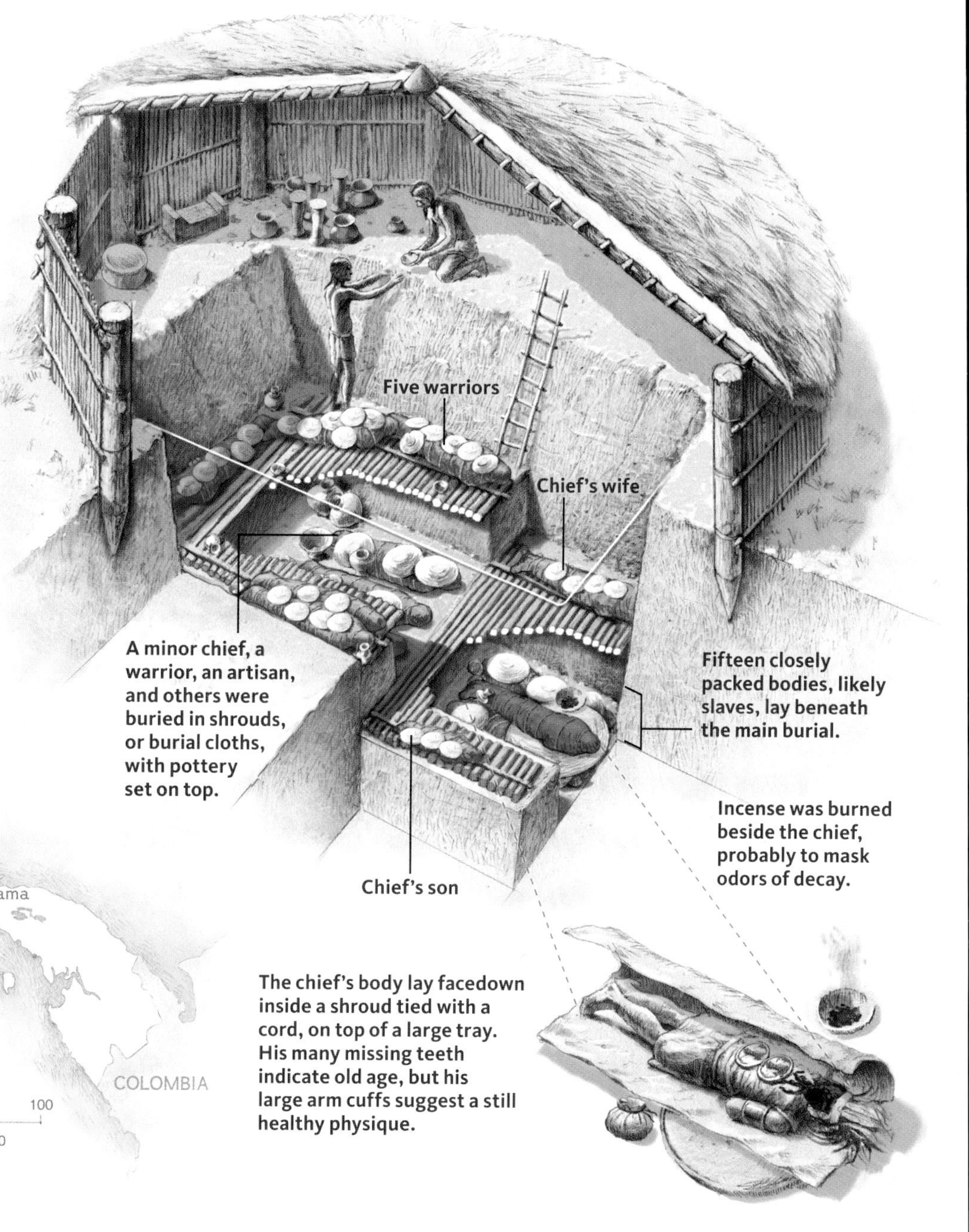

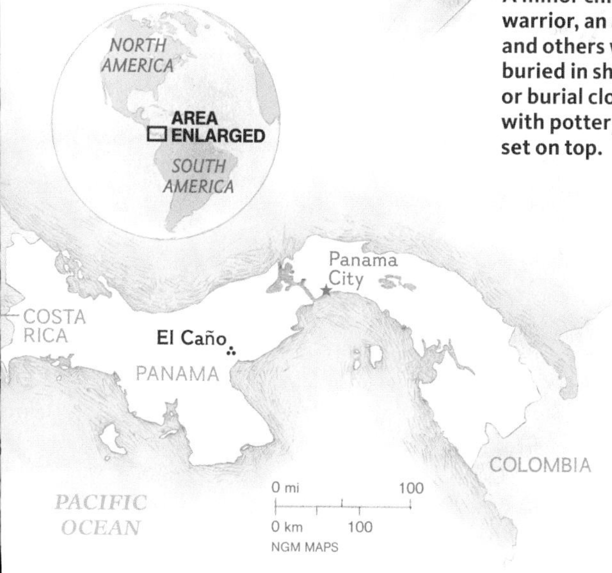

TOMB GOLD

1. This ornament was unearthed during an excavation at Sitio Conte in 1940.
2. This seahorse pendant was among the personal treasures found in a chief's tomb at El Caño.

1

2

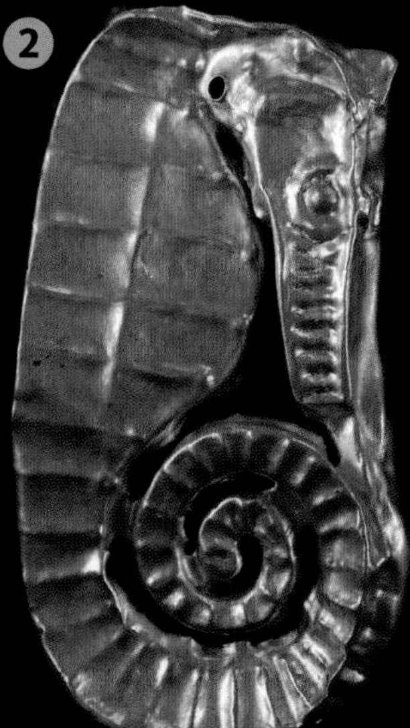

HIGH CRAFTSMANSHIP
This dramatic gold plaque from Sitio Conte shows that artisans in Panama were creating complex and skillful works.

nothing like the attractions that have drawn scientists to the Maya territory. There is no lasting architecture and no evidence of advanced culture, such as a calendar. Heat and humidity have rotted away ancient shelters that were made of bamboo and thatch. The only everyday items that remain are broken pottery and stone tools.

BACK TO EL CAÑO

Along the same river that flows by the Sitio Conte cemetery, a line of tall **monoliths** crosses a field near El Caño. In 1925 the stones attracted an American adventurer named Hyatt Verrill. He dug several rough holes nearby, uncovering three skeletons. Further excavations found several modest graves, but they turned up no treasure.

Despite those unpromising results, Julia Mayo had a good feeling about this site. As a research associate at the Smithsonian Tropical Research Institute in Panama City, she had studied Lothrop's report on Sitio Conte. She knew he had found monoliths as well as graves, and she thought there might be a connection. If she was right, more burials of warrior chiefs from that same culture would be waiting underground at El Caño. It was just a question of figuring out where they might lie.

Her initial survey picked up traces of a slightly raised circle about 260 feet in diameter. Guessing it was the border of a cemetery, she started digging at dead center. She guessed right. The artifacts now coming to light confirm that the Spanish descriptions of this region are generally reliable. Sitio Conte was not the only place where treasure would be found.

Specialists at the Smithsonian Institution began to study the materials unearthed by Mayo's team and soon made a major discovery. Impurities in the gold suggest that the metal was mined in the region. Experts no longer believe that Panama's treasures were imported from farther south, where cultures were supposedly older and more advanced. The people in this area may have lived in simple huts, but they were rich enough to support master craftsmen. They were also cultured enough to enjoy fine art. This was a new perspective on the region's early history.

Mayo believes her cemetery holds about 20 more tombs of chiefs like the two she has excavated. When she estimates how long it would take to uncover them all, the number is so extreme it sounds like a joke. Her team of ten works slowly and painstakingly. Bit by bit, they scrap back the hard soil to gather the smallest pieces of evidence. In four years they have exposed two percent of the cemetery. If work were to continue at that pace, it would take 196 years to finish the job. So there's no danger of running out of work to do at El Caño.

During the digging season, as Mayo and her team eat lunch on the shady porch of El Caño's small museum, they look out across hundreds of acres of sugarcane. Mayo believes it's all fertile ground for archaeology.

Just a few miles upriver from El Caño, in fact, Mayo has found signs of another cemetery. If it's as rich as El Caño and Sitio Conte, one day this area may be compared to Egypt's Valley of the Kings, where dozens of ancient Egyptian rulers were buried in rich tombs. In Egypt, though, most of the tombs have been looted. Here they should still be full of surprises.

THINK ABOUT IT!

1 **Sequence Events** What discoveries led Julia Mayo to begin investigating the site at El Caño?

2 **Draw Conclusions** Why did Samuel Lothrop think the gold found at Sitio Conte dated from the period of the Spanish conquistadors?

BACKGROUND & VOCABULARY

ceramics *n.* (suh-RA-mihks) objects made of clay that have been dried and hardened at a high temperature

conquistador *n.* (kon-KEES-tuh-dor) a 16th-century Spanish soldier or leader who conquered lands in North and South America

geophysical *adj.* (JEE-uh-FIH-zih-kuhl) relating to physical features on and below Earth's surface

monolith *n.* (MAH-nuh-lihth) a large stone set up as a monument

The 3,500 pieces of treasure unearthed in Staffordshire, England, in 2009 were mostly gold adornments for war gear. Who buried them and why?

NOT YOUR EVERYDAY FIELD

One day in the late seventh century an unknown party traveled along an old Roman road through a forest in the Anglo-Saxon kingdom of Mercia, in the land that is now called England. They might have been soldiers or thieves, but they were certainly not casual travelers. Stepping off the road, they dug a pit and buried a stash of treasure in the ground.

Magical Mystery Treasure

Adapted from "Magical Mystery Treasure," by Caroline Alexander, in *National Geographic,* November 2011

RIDING TO WAR
Warriors from noble famlies, like the man in this painting, carried finely crafted swords into battle. Centuries later, a collection of these weapons was unearthed in England.

Thirteen hundred years later, treasure hunters with metal detectors came by and asked farmer Fred Johnson for permission to walk that same stretch of land, which now belonged to him. "I told one I'd lost a wrench and asked him to find that," Johnson says. They never found the wrench. Instead, they told Johnson that Anglo-Saxon treasure was buried in his pasture.

The discovery of the Staffordshire Hoard, as it was called, shocked scholars who study early English history as well as the general public. Great discoveries had been made in ancient burial sites, but the treasure found in Johnson's field was different. The quality and style of the gold, silver, and garnet objects were extraordinary. Some compared them to the legendary Book of Kells, an illustrated manuscript created by monks around A.D. 800 and considered to be one of Ireland's national treasures.

Once catalogued, the hoard was found to contain about 3,500 pieces. The items followed a striking pattern—the 300 sword-**hilt** fittings, 92 sword-**pommel** caps, and 10 **scabbard** pendants all had military uses. There were no coins or jewelry, and only three religious objects. Also, many of the items seemed to have been bent or broken. This treasure, then, was a pile of broken military hardware hidden 13 centuries ago in a region that was often fought over by neighboring kingdoms. The Staffordshire Hoard was historic, but also very puzzling.

A HISTORY OF INVASIONS

For centuries people from mainland Europe—such as the Celts, Romans, Vikings, and Normans—came and went, leaving their mark on Britain's landscape. But the six centuries of Anglo-Saxon rule, from around A.D. 410 to the Norman Conquest in 1066, is the time that most defines modern England.

Germanic tribes had been moving across Europe since the third century, and some may have entered Britain at that time. In the third century, Britain was under the control of the Roman Empire. In the early fifth century the Germanic tribes threatened Rome, forcing it to remove its troops from Britain to defend the capital. As the Romans left, tribes from the west and north of Britain poured across the borders. Around 450, the Britons (the native people of Britain) brought in Germanic soldiers to help fight off these tribes. Bede, an eighth century historian, said these warriors were from "three very powerful Germanic tribes, the Saxons, Angles, and Jutes." Their homelands were in Germany, the Netherlands, and Denmark. The word Anglo-Saxon comes from the names of the first two tribes.

The first Germanic soldiers told of the richness of the land and the "slackness of the Britons." Soon, the Angles, Saxons, and Jutes turned on their former allies the Britons. Bede noted that "hordes of these peoples eagerly crowded into the island and the number of foreigners began to increase to such an extent that they became a source of terror to the natives."

Most of the surviving native Britons fled or were enslaved. Some, however, adopted Germanic fashions, and native British culture was influenced by the Anglo-Saxons. The most important legacy of the Anglo-Saxons is probably the English language. Much of Europe emerged from the post-Roman world speaking Spanish, French, or other languages derived from Latin, the language of the Romans. But the language of England would be Germanic.

BURIED TREASURES

The discovery of a treasure hoard in an English field was not unusual. Coins, weapons, and even a silver dinner service have been found in the soil. The tradition of burying treasure is even mentioned in the Anglo-Saxon **epic** *Beowulf.* In the tale, the warrior king Beowulf battled a dragon that was guarding gold and "garnered jewels" buried in the ground.

Anglo-Saxons buried treasure for many reasons, often to hide it from an invading enemy. At other times, it might be a religious offering. But the Staffordshire Hoard is neither

of those. The first clue is the nature of the hoard, which reflects the militarism of the Germanic tribes. This warlike nature impressed the Romans. The Roman historian Tacitus noted that "they conduct no business, public or private, except under arms." When a boy came of age he was presented with a shield and spear.

Warfare and alliances were the likely origin of the tribal kingships of early Anglo-Saxon England. Mercia was among the most important of these kingships, and one of the most warlike. Between 600 and 850 Mercia fought at least 43 wars with its neighbors, more than half with Wessex and Wales.

The long cutting sword was an important Germanic weapon. Its blade was pattern welded—made from twisted rods and strips of iron hammered together. The polished blades rippled with zigzag patterns. One sixth century witness said the great swords appeared "to be grained with tiny snakes, and here such varied shadows play that you would believe the shining metal to be interwoven with many colors."

There are 92 sword pommels in the Staffordshire Hoard. This is about the same number as men in a nobleman's troop of **retainers**. The hoard, then, could be the military gear belonging to a lord's elite troops. Often a sword was issued by a lord to each of his retainers. It was returned if the retainer died before his lord did. Otherwise, swords were often buried with the warrior or kept by the family as an heirloom.

But sometimes swords and other valuable objects were buried on their own. That is, they were not buried for safekeeping, but as part of a ritual. "We can no longer see hoards only as piggy banks," says Kevin Leahy, an expert on Anglo-Saxon history. Many

ART OF WAR
Terry Herbert displays treasures he found in Fred Johnson's field. He holds up a piece of a helmet that was copied in an artist's recreation of the full helmet to the left.

The $5.3 Million Hoard

GOLDEN TREASURES

1. This strip of gold with biblical verses on both sides was also once crowned with a gem.
2. This sword hilt is decorated with precisely cut garnet.
3. This delicately worked fragment was a cheek protector from a warrior's helmet.
4. These items from the hoard may have been bent or broken to fit into a small space as part of a ritual, or for some other purpose.

3

2

1

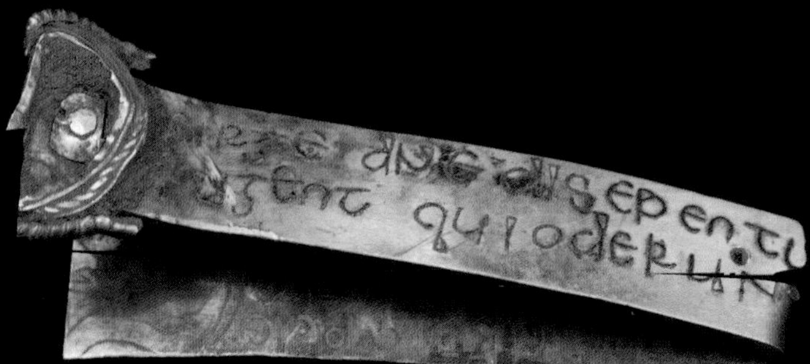

4

weapons, like the objects in the hoard, were bent or broken before they were buried.

"This is a hoard for male display," says historian Nicholas Brooks. He calls the objects found in Staffordshire "bling for warrior companions of the king." Gold makes up nearly 75 percent of the metal in the hoard, but according to Brooks, "the source is a mystery." The origin of most gold in England was Roman coins. Imperial gold currency had been taken by Germanic tribes following the sack of Rome in the fifth century. By the time of the Staffordshire Hoard, however, gold supplies were dwindling.

Historian Guy Halsall has estimated the value of the hoard's gold at about $5.3 million in today's dollars. In its own time, however, the hoard's worth was surely affected by other factors. Gold dazzles, but the most valuable part of the weaponry was "the long, sharp, pointy bit you killed people with," as Halsall notes. And sword blades were not present in the hoard. Possibly, they were kept to reuse.

SACRED OBJECTS

It is important to keep in mind that the pieces in the hoard were created and buried by people who believed in magic. Germanic myths tell of the gods' great hall of gold. Nordic tales mention magical objects, such as the hammer carried by the god Thor. So a gold object believed to have magical powers might be more prized than a gold coin, which only had monetary value.

This belief may also explain the only three nonmilitary objects in the Staffordshire Hoard: two gold crosses and a strip of gold inscribed with a bible quotation. The cross was a useful symbol known to have been used in actual battles. Bede tells of the preparations King Oswald made before a battle against the Welsh in 634. He "set up the sign of the holy cross and, on bended knees, prayed God to send heavenly aid to His worshippers in their dire need." He and his men then "gained the victory that their faith merited." The strip of gold inscribed with a biblical quotation may also have been used as a good luck charm. The inscription reads, "Rise up, Lord, may your enemies be dispersed and those who hate you flee from your face."

The Mercians were border raiders. "The hoard was found on a frontier zone, which is always interesting," Kevin Leahy says. "It was on the border between Mercia and Wales." In other words, it was in contested territory. Around 650, a battle was fought there involving Mercia and Wales. Much plunder was carried away, possibly down the road near where the Staffordshire Hoard was found.

There are other possible theories. The hoard may have been buried in a spot where it was easy to recover later. Or it might have been an offering, never meant to be found. It may also have been ransom, or booty, or a collection of heirlooms buried at a later time.

Today, the hoard burial site is a grassy field where Fred Johnson grazes horses. Odds are we will never know the story behind the Staffordshire Hoard. But in a world that no longer believes in magic spells, would we understand it if we did?

THINK ABOUT IT!

1 **Draw Conclusions** What does the military nature of the objects found in the Staffordshire Hoard tell about the people who may have buried them?

2 **Form and Support Opinions** The Staffordshire Hoard was found on land belonging to Fred Johnson. Do you think he should have been allowed to keep it? Why or why not?

BACKGROUND & VOCABULARY

epic *n.* (EH-pihk) a long narrative poem, often about a hero

hilt *n.* (HIHLT) the handle of a sword

pommel *n.* (PAH-muhl) the knob at the bottom of a sword's hilt

retainer *n.* (rih-TAY-nuhr) a personal servant

scabbard *n.* (SKA-burd) a protective case for a sword's blade

RESCUED
This exquisitely detailed gold figurine of a ram was discovered in Afghanistan in 1978. It has survived thanks to those who hid it from looters during dangerous times.

Afghanistan's *Hidden Treasures*

Adapted from "Afghanistan's Hidden Treasures,"
by Roger Atwood, in *National Geographic*, June 2008

Concealed from invaders and feared lost, a collection of precious artifacts reveals the rich cultures that came together at one of history's great crossroads. For a country shattered by decades of war, evidence of a glorious past inspires a sense of national pride.

KEEPING THE SECRET

Omara Khan Massoudi, director of the National Museum of Afghanistan, knows how to keep a secret. In the 1980s, Massoudi saw his country sliding into war and decided to do something to protect his museum's treasures. So he and a few trusted colleagues secretly hid them away for safekeeping.

First, Afghanistan was invaded by the Soviet Union in 1979. Ten years later, civil war reduced much of Kabul, the country's capital, to ruins. As Afghan warlords battled for control, fighters pillaged the museum. They sold the best artifacts on the black market and used museum records to light campfires. In 1994 the roof and top floor of the building were destroyed. And then in 2001 teams of **Taliban** fighters smashed 2,000 artifacts that they felt insulted their religion.

Through those dark years, Massoudi and a few other museum officials kept quiet about their hoard of museum artifacts. The most precious cultural treasures—including valuable pieces made of gold—remained hidden in vaults under the presidential palace. Researchers the world over thought the objects were lost forever. They feared they had been destroyed by the Taliban or sold to dishonest antique dealers.

By October 2003, two years after the Taliban were driven from power, most of Massoudi's colleagues had disappeared or fled. He was ready to find out if the objects had survived the war. To everyone's great relief, all the gold was there. Later, researchers opened a set of lockers in the same vault and made another wonderful discovery. The lockers contained priceless 2,000-year-old ivory carvings and glassware that had been unearthed near the city of Begram. Massoudi's staff had hidden those, too. They also were remarkably well preserved.

"If we had not hidden them, the treasures of Afghanistan would have been lost. That is a fact. Those who knew the truth kept silent," says Massoudi, sipping tea in his office.

RECOVERED TREASURES

Afghanistan's museum has been rebuilt with international help, and it hums with activity now. Exhibit planners walk the galleries, taking measurements for future shows. Teachers lecture to groups of schoolgirls in head scarves. At the door, policemen keep a close watch. Visitor numbers have increased to about 6,000 a year. Storerooms are filling with looted artifacts intercepted by customs agents all over the world.

Over 5,000 are from Switzerland and Denmark alone. A warehouse in London holds more than four tons of illegally exported Afghan artifacts seized by British police, waiting to be returned.

In the museum lobby, Massoudi shows what it means to rebuild heritage. Standing in a display case is a life-size statue of a Buddhist deity, dating from the third century A.D., when Afghanistan was mostly Buddhist. Taliban hammers had shattered the statue, but patient workers had reassembled it. Cracks remain, but the statue's face glows with joy and peace once again.

"As we finish the restoration of pieces, we bring them out to show the public, one by one. We will be doing this for many years," says Massoudi. Yet the best artifacts, hidden for so long, won't be seen in Kabul for a while. The museum needs better security. Recent bombings around Kabul show that risks remain.

Faced with these problems, Afghans gathered their dazzling treasures into an exhibition and sent it on an international tour. The Afghan government asked National Geographic to help organize an exhibition that toured Europe before coming to Washington, D.C. Besides safeguarding their treasures, Afghans hope the exhibit will improve their country's image.

"The history of Afghanistan is one of receiving the arts of others, and then turning them into our own way of expression," says Massoudi. He believes the exhibit will help people see beyond his country's recent history of intolerance and isolation. For centuries before the more recent conflicts, Afghanistan was a creative melting pot and center of international trade.

A RICH HERITAGE

Walk through the bazaars in Kabul and you'll see how Afghanistan became known as the crossroads of Asia. European, Arab, Indian, and Chinese faces are seen side by side. Over the centuries people came from everywhere and left behind "some of the most remarkable archaeological finds in all of Central Asia," says Fredrik Hiebert of the National Geographic Society. (For more on Fredrik Hiebert, see "Explorer's Journal," on pages 5–11.)

Many of the brilliant objects came from the ancient city of Begram, about 40 miles from Kabul. Today land mines litter the countryside and American fighter jets fly overhead. But 2,000 years ago this was the prosperous summer capital of the far-flung Kushan Empire. Traders brought ivory and art to Begram from all over the known world. Travelers snacked on local figs and grapes against the backdrop of the majestic, snowy peaks of the **Hindu Kush**.

AFGHAN GOLD

All these items were locked away in a vault by Massoudi and his associates.

1. **An ornament of gold and imitation turquoise**
2. **A golden crown found at Tillya Tepe**
3. **A gold and turquoise sword hilt from the Afghan National Museum**
4. **Two identical gold bracelets with lion heads**

1
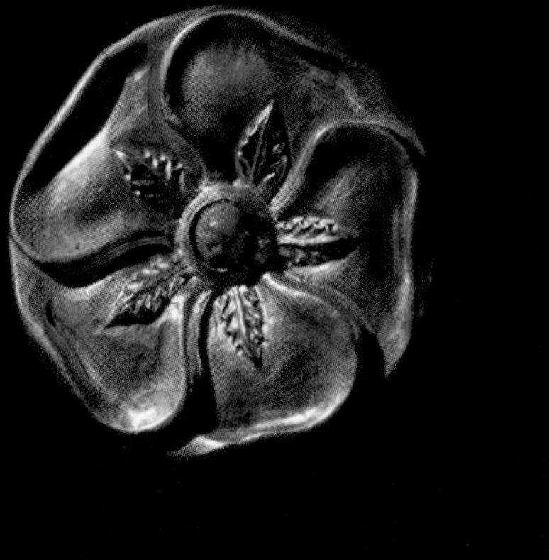

2

French archaeologists began excavating the Begram site in the late 1930s. They found a wealth of luxury goods suggesting a thriving trade economy at the time Rome was in decline. There were bronze sculptures from Italy, **lacquer** boxes from China, and plaster medallions from Greece. They also found beautifully painted Egyptian glass vessels depicting the great lighthouse at the city of Alexandria and an African leopard hunt. Among the most impressive objects were more than 1,000 carved ivory and bone sculptures of smiling women and mythical river creatures typical of Indian art.

Someone abandoned this stunning collection inside two walled-in rooms around A.D. 200. Archaeologists at first thought the structure was the ruins of a royal home. Researchers now think it was a warehouse for luxury goods being shipped across Asia.

Like Begram, Tillya Tepe (which means "golden hill") in northwestern Afghanistan yielded treasures, including the gold objects Massoudi later hid. Discovered by a Russian archaeologist in the 1970s, the hoard tells the story of how nomads arrived from Central Asia and created an Afghan style that was a mixture of East and West. From the wilds of Siberia comes a bear depicted on a knife handle, dancing with a grapevine in its mouth. A golden Aphrodite with wings shows the impact of Greek culture. But she also has an Indian-style circle on her forehead, showing Hindu influences.

Archaeology is slowly returning to Afghanistan, bringing more discoveries and deeper knowledge. New sites are being excavated, and old ones are being revisited. In the past, American or European researchers played key roles. These days, Afghan archaeologists are often the project leaders.

On a steep hillside outside Kabul, Afghan researchers are working at a fifth century Buddhist site called Tepe Maranjan. There they found the remains of 16 clay **bodhisattvas** (bod-dih-SAHT-vuhz) arranged in a circle. Only their feet and the bottom of their robes escaped damage. They were probably demolished in the first Islamic invasions a few centuries after they were created. Also gone, except for its bare feet, was a 20-foot-tall Buddha that had towered over the site. Perched on a dry hilltop overlooking the plains, the site would have been a quiet place for the Buddhist practice of meditation.

"If this had been discovered during the Taliban's day, it might well have been destroyed," says archaeologist Najib Sedeqi. Guards watch the site carefully, and neighbors help out.

Every period in the country's history is being opened up to exploration. Archaeologists will

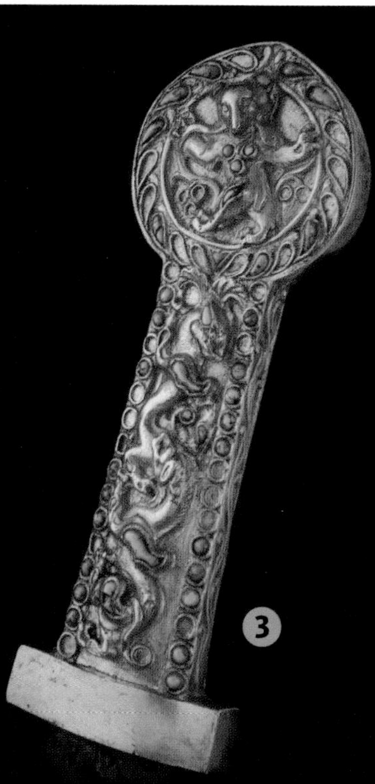

3

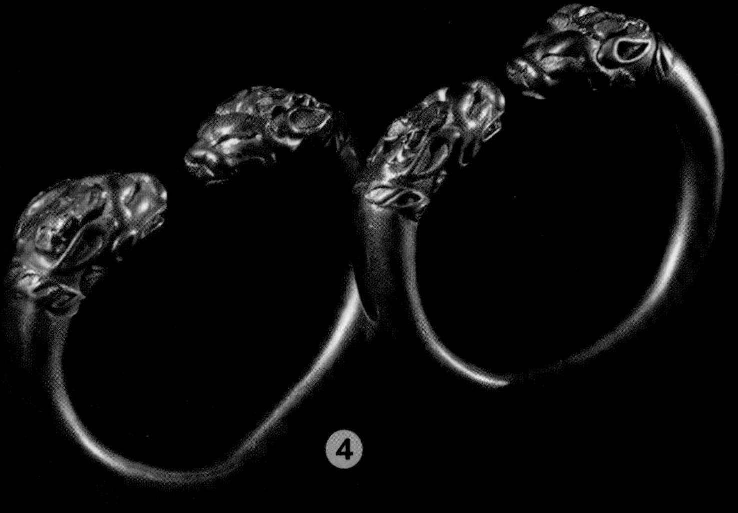

4

soon start excavating one of the oldest mosques in Afghanistan, near the city of Balkh. With its mighty columns and thick walls the mosque expresses power and stability. When Islam came to Afghanistan, it clearly came to stay.

BROUGHT TO LIGHT This stone figure from the third or fourth century A.D. was one of 2,000 artifacts broken by the Taliban.

PROTECTING A LEGACY

Despite the progress, huge challenges remain. Crime and looting are a constant threat to Afghanistan's cultural revival. At Tillya Tepe villagers looking for building materials and valuable antiquities have almost leveled the "golden hill." At Ai Khanum, where Alexander the Great built a city, archaeologists found baths and **Hellenic** lettering—traces of Greek culture on the doorstep of China. Since then, looters started to pillage the site, turning it into a bleak landscape of pits and tunnels. At Begram, they have become bolder and better equipped.

"We were patrolling the site one evening when we heard a gunshot, and then I realized that we were the target," said Aynadin Sodeqi. He commands a new Begram police unit formed to protect archaeological sites. Sodeqi and his men had stumbled upon a group of looters digging up treasures to sell. The looters escaped, but Sodeqi and his men found at least part of their stash. It included 28 ancient coins and a stone tablet decorated with lotus flowers. Sodeqi also found a piece of equipment the looters may have planned to use. What kind of equipment? He acted out his answer, holding out his fists and vibrating them up and down: a jackhammer.

"The looters know the value of the things they pillage," says Nadir Rassouli, director of Afghanistan's Institute of Archaeology. "They are armed, and no matter how many officers we place at sites, they attack them and drive them off. Then they loot."

At Rassouli's suggestion, the Afghan government created the archaeology police force in 2004. It has 500 men, but Rassouli says it would take many more to cover the entire country. Most lack training and weapons. The first sustained attack on the new force came in 2006 near the city of Balkh. Four officers were killed, and at least six more have been killed on duty since then.

Tons of Afghan loot have been taken out of the country. Coins are particularly popular, and Begram has long been known as the place to find them. A British traveler in 1833 reported that local people dug up 30,000 coins every year. He carried off 2,000 himself.

Today it is land mines left over from the wars that are buried in Begram's fields. Among fragments of ancient pottery, lines of red stones warn of danger. A closer look reveals innocent-looking plastic disks lurking in the grass like discarded toys. Such is the poverty and desperation that not even land mines will stop looters.

Afghans are trying to put their country back together but face many obstacles. Land mines, suicide bombs, and the memories of recent war all take their toll. "The biggest thing that's broken in Afghanistan isn't the buildings, or the roads, or even the electrical system. It's the broken psychology," says Hiebert. "Twenty-five years of war is hell. Not only were tons of artifacts stolen, so was the Afghans' history, their heritage. Afghan children no longer know Afghan folk songs. How can they get their pride back?"

There are many answers to that question. One can be seen in Kabul, where an Afghan national treasure is getting a makeover. In the early 1500s, the Mogul emperor Babur planted a 20-acre garden with his favorite trees. His garden had been neglected for years when the Aga Khan Trust for Culture began restoring it. It is now Kabul's finest public park and a glowing symbol of Afghanistan's renewal.

Babur's restored white-marble tomb stands at the top of the garden. Not far away, there is a full-size reproduction of a caravansary, a lodge where caravans would spend the night. Builders have erected it on the same spot where one stood in Babur's time. Sometimes the courtyard echoes with the haunting sounds of a traditional stringed instrument known as the sarinda.

CULTURAL HERO Massoudi examines a statue that had been damaged by the Taliban and was later reconstructed.

Kaka Qader often plays there. He is one of Afghanistan's few remaining sarinda masters. But he won't be the last. A bright-eyed music student watches as the master plays. Then the young man takes the instrument, and a tabla drummer joins in. The courtyard fills with the hopeful sound of a new generation of Afghans playing their music.

THINK ABOUT IT!

1 **Draw Conclusions** Why did Omara Khan Massoudi's colleagues disappear or flee when the Taliban took over Afghanistan?

2 **Summarize** How did Massoudi and his colleagues protect Afghanistan's national treasures?

3 **Identify Problems and Solutions** What obstacles must Afghans overcome to restore their rich culture? In what ways are they putting their country back together?

BACKGROUND & VOCABULARY

bodhisattva *n.* (boh-dih-SAHT-vuh) a Buddhist teacher or holy man

Hellenic *adj.* (heh-LEH-nihk) of or relating to the culture of the ancient Greeks

Hindu Kush *n.* (HIN-doo KUSH) a mountain range in central Afghanistan

lacquer *n.* (LAK-ur) a type of shiny, colorful varnish

Taliban *n.* (TAHL-ih-ban) The Taliban took power in Afghanistan in the mid-1990s. The Taliban practice an extremely conservative form of Islam and sought to destroy cultural artifacts they deemed not Islamic.

Document-Based Question

Archaeologists work in some of the most remote locations on Earth—and the most uncomfortable. Excavation sites can take them to scorching deserts, churning seas, and even the smelly sewers of Rome. It takes a special kind of person to become an archaeologist—one with a deep curiosity about our shared past and someone who is willing to endure challenges.

DOCUMENT 1 Primary Source

Working Against Time

National Geographic Explorer Mark Aldenderfer is an archaeologist who has excavated sites all over the world. In this excerpt from an interview with National Geographic, he talks about discovering a piece of 4,000-year-old gold jewelry in Peru—the earliest gold jewelry found in the Americas to date—on a stormy November day.

> [It] turned out to be a gold necklace around the base of a skull of a woman. Not only was this wholly [completely] unexpected, it created a major challenge to get it out of the ground before the storm arrived and before too much attention had been drawn to the discovery. We feared that had the local villagers been made aware of the necklace, the site would have been looted overnight. We managed to get the burial out of the ground and the gold safely back to the lab before the storm hit and its existence was widely known.

from www.nationalgeographic.com/explorers/bios/mark-aldenderfer

CONSTRUCTED RESPONSE

1. What challenges did Aldenderfer and his team face when they tried to get the gold jewelry out of the ground?

DOCUMENT 2 Secondary Source

Diving for Artifacts

Underwater archaeologist and National Geographic Explorer Guillermo de Anda searches for Maya ruins in deep, remote caves. These caves had a great deal of religious significance for the Maya, so they sometimes built temples in them. The following describes how de Anda spends a typical day exploring the dangerous, hard-to-reach caves.

> "Exploring these caves is very demanding," he admits. "The ancient Maya like to make it hard; they searched for extremely distant places. So we know the harder it is to get there, the better our findings may be." De Anda's team of four disappears into caves for 12 or more hours at a time, draped with equipment, hacking apart overgrown entrances, rappelling [descending using ropes] down 100-foot vertical drops, diving into 200-foot pools, swimming horizontally along narrow passageways, squeezing through tiny openings, dodging swarms of bats, crawling on floors moving with snakes and scorpions, and never forgetting how to find their way out.

from www.nationalgeographic.com/explorers/bios/guillermo-de-anda-alanis

CONSTRUCTED RESPONSE

2. Why does de Anda welcome difficulties when he's searching for Maya ruins?

What challenges and triumphs do archaeologists experience in their work?

DOCUMENT 3 Primary Source

Archaeologist at Work

Archaeological work isn't always adventurous. Once an artifact is removed from an excavation site, it must be handled very carefully. In this photo, an archaeologist in a lab uses a brush to carefully clean a sherd of pottery recovered from a Dutch ship that sank off the tip of South America.

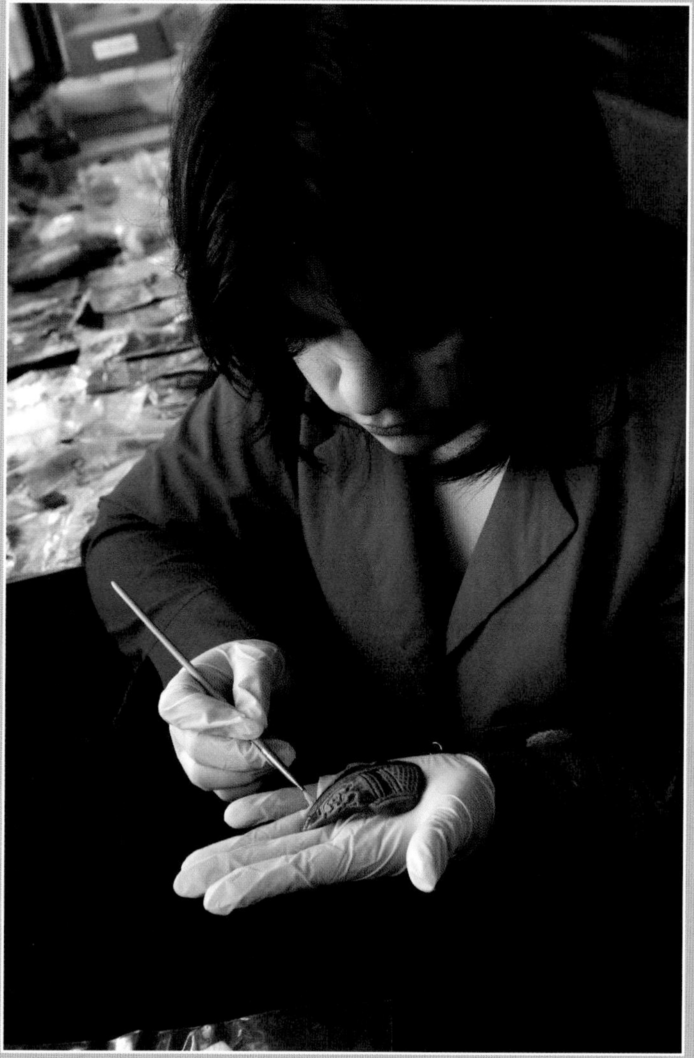

CONSTRUCTED RESPONSE

3. What qualities are needed to perform the work illustrated in the photo?

PUT IT TOGETHER

Review Think about your responses to the three questions and what you have learned about archaeology and the work of archaeologists.

Categorize Create a two-column chart. Use it to list challenges and triumphs the archaeologists you have read about have faced. Use information from the documents and articles you have read.

Write What challenges and triumphs do archaeologists experience in their work? Write a paragraph based on the information in your chart to discuss the work of archaeologists.

INDEX

SKILLS